Interpreting the Present Time

[Jesus] said to the crowds, " When you see a cloud rising in the west, you immediately say, 'It is going to rain'; and so it happens. And when you see the south wind blowing, you say, 'There will be scorching heat'; and it happens. You hypocrites! You know how to interpret the appearance of earth and sky, but why do you not know how to interpret the present time? And why do you not judge for yourselves what is right?''

(Luke 12:54–57)

Interpreting the Present Time

History, the Bible, and the
Church's Mission Today

Cyril H. Powles

Anglican Book Centre
Toronto, Canada

1994
Anglican Book Centre
600 Jarvis Street
Toronto, Ontario
Canada M4Y 2J6

Typesetting by Jay Tee Graphics Ltd.

Canadian Cataloguing in Publication Data

Powles, Cyril Hamilton, 1918-
   Interpreting the present time: history, the
Bible, and the Church's mission today

ISBN 1-55126-094-8

1. Mission of the church. I. Title.

BV601.8.P68 1994   260   C94-931508-7

Contents

Preface

Many influences have combined to shape the ideas which follow. They begin with growing up in a missionary household and continue with life formed as a student in the exciting atmosphere of the Student Christian Movement. Out of the latter involvement came a collaboration of nearly fifty years with Marjorie, whose free and questioning mind has always probed into places which my more easy-going temperament was content to ignore. Her combination of radical honesty with clear-sighted realism has influenced my thinking so fundamentally that it has become difficult to say which of us was the originator of any given statement. So you will find my indebtedness to her throughout this essay.

Shortly after our marriage in 1946 and going to Japan in 1949, I discovered David Paton's little book, *Christian Missions and the Judgment of God*. Through him I learned about Roland Allen, and used the ideas in the latter author's provocative writings as the basis of a seminar on mission held in Tokyo during the fifties. Teaching history, particularly examining the history of Christianity outside the Western world, has left an indelible impression on my understanding. I have learned as much from third-world students in my classes as I have taught them.

Discussions with many people have further shaped those ideas. The comradeship which surrounded the liturgical activism of the Society of the Catholic Commonwealth remains to this day, forming the basis for concepts such as the counter-cultural community and its eucharistic spirituality. Working papers, written to stimulate thinking and discussion in the Anglican church's World Mission Subcommittee (now the Partners in World Mission Committee) and a local area conference of the Primate's World Relief and Development Fund, pushed the ideas forward a little more, as did the comments resulting from publication of some of the papers. Colleagues—Tom Anthony, Terry Brown, and Chris Lind, to name only three—have read earlier drafts and supplied help-ful criticism for which many thanks are due. The symposium which the latter two edited, *Justice as Mission*, contains essays which relate closely to my subject. Chapter 2 of the present work began as a lecture delivered in Japan under the Channing Moore Williams Lectureship of the Nippon Seikokai.

With a theme like "Interpreting the Present Time," it is dif-ficult to keep up with times that are changing so quickly. So, though what follows is in many ways a group effort, I must accept sole responsibility for ideas or interpretations that are mistaken or out of date.

It is my hope that this book may prove useful for congrega-tional study. Following the first two, introductory chapters, a good deal of Bible study is involved, so the text can best be read with a Bible handy to check the references. As group discussion formed part of the original composition, so also the present text can be used more profitably by groups where reading is frequently inter-rupted by discussion. I pray that the ideas contained in this essay may in some small way contribute to thought and action on the part of the People of God during this Decade of Evangelism.

Cyril Powles,
Toronto, 1994.

N. B. Most of the passages quoted in the following text have been taken from the New Revised Standard Version of the Bible (NRSV), but I have felt free to alter some texts in consultation with the original Hebrew or Greek when the context seemed to call for it or a more inclusive rendering could be made. At the end of each chapter a short list of articles and books, easily obtaina-ble in a religious book shop or library, has been appended. There are also a few questions for use as discussion starters.

1   Crisis in Mission

Christianity's mission in the world today faces a crisis. In every age such crises have arisen and new movements have emerged within the church, under the guidance of the Holy Spirit, calling people to follow Jesus Christ in witnessing to God's love for humankind. In the early church, when Christians became too closely identified with the doubtful blessings offered by the Roman state, the monastic movement reminded them of Jesus' world-denying thirst for righteousness and the coming of God's rule on earth. Such reform movements have recurred regularly throughout history, reminding Christians that God's mission is never complete. The leaders of the Protestant Reformation reflected this belief when they adopted the slogan *Ecclesia semper reformanda* (The church must always be reformed). And Jesus emphasized this open-ended view of the Christian mission when he taught us to pray constantly, "May your rule be established (Thy kingdom come); your will be done on earth as it is in heaven."

One aspect of the contemporary crisis is the perception that the great missionary movement, which began in our modern Western world, to make the Good News of God's love in Jesus Christ known throughout the earth, appears to have run down. With the possible exception of some conservative evangelicals, fewer and fewer people are offering themselves for overseas service. In Japan, where my wife and I worked for over twenty years, the decline began as early as 1956. By 1985 the trend had become worldwide. Offerings for missions declined, although they were somewhat balanced by increased contributions to such humanitarian enterprises as OXFAM and the Primate's World Relief and Development Fund (PWRDF) of the Anglican church.

Surveys, such as the study by Reginald Bibby entitled *Fragmented Gods*, suggest that Canadians see the church primarily as an organization placed in the local community to serve their needs, rather than as the body of those who have been called to follow Christ by living a changed life. As with the supermarket, they want the local parish to be there whenever they want to call on it: to baptize their children and marry them when they grow up; to counsel them in trouble and bury them when they die. A few will attend a Sunday service (especially on the great feasts such as Christmas or Easter), but they see that as a time of quiet or celebration, when they can escape from the everyday world of competition, strife, and change. So, naturally, they do not welcome sermons which disturb that quiet by raising issues related to the outside world such as the Christian's mission, or the abolition of poverty and injustice.

Even the minority of Canadians who go to church regularly and take their faith seriously find it difficult to make up their minds exactly how the church's mission is to be conducted. For some, the old ideas no longer seem to work. The ties in the past of overseas missions with imperialism make them feel guilty, while a closer contact with non-Christian religions makes a mission aimed simplistically at proselytizing problematic. Yet neither are they satisfied to substitute for it a program of vague humanitarianism which seems always in danger of spilling over into paternalism. Many of us gaze with envy at what seems like the simple faith of the conservative evangelicals who still follow what they firmly believe to be *The Gospel* with its Great Commission to go and make disciples of all nations, baptizing them in the name of the Father, and of the Son, and of the Holy Ghost. Have we somehow fallen away from the faith of our ancestors?

Before we can answer that question, however, we must review in some detail what has come to be called the "traditional" view of mission. (I have put the term in quotation marks because this is actually a view which gained full acceptance among non-Roman Catholics less than two hundred years ago—a short period in the two-thousand-year-old history of Christianity—when the English Baptist, William Carey, wrote his stirring tract, *An Enquiry into the Obligation of Christians to Use Means for the Conversion of the Heathen.*) To summarize this view, the modern missionary movement which carried out the great expansion of Christianity from post-medieval Europe and America operated on the basis of four broad assumptions:

1. It was responding to the command of Jesus (the Great Commission), "Go ye into all the world and preach the gospel to every creature" (Mark 16:15; also Matthew 28:19 and Luke 24:47).

2. It was the duty of all Christians to obey that command, but it could be fulfilled in different ways. By a convenient kind of division of labour, overseas service was seen as the special vocation of an elite group, the missionaries, while ordinary Christians could obey by supporting overseas work with money and prayer.

3. The world was divided into two large geographical areas: Christendom, whose belief and culture were Christian, and Heathendom, whose inhabitants lived in constant danger of eternal damnation if they did not have the gospel preached to them. In the tradition of the medieval Crusades, mission was seen as territorial expansion through the conquest of Heathendom (think of all the military language in those old missionary hymns!). Usually such expansion was seen in terms of the organized outreach of an institutional church which was transplanted, with all its (Western) cultural accoutrements, onto the new soil.

4. Expansion took place by means of the conversion of individuals. Conversion was seen primarily as a person's rejection of the old idols and the acceptance of Jesus Christ as Lord and Saviour, the One who atoned for their sins by his death. The new life was expressed in otherworldly terms as the plucking of an individual soul out of a sinful world (the old, "heathen" culture) and preparing him/her for heaven by introduction into the "Christian" life of the church.

The above assumptions were held within a context of a highly complex pattern of economic, political, and ideological forces which were continually shifting their relation to one another as societies developed. At the risk of oversimplification, however, it can be said that almost all missionary enterprises in the Western world since the end of the Middle Ages began within the context of some prior commercial or colonial commitment on the part of the nations in which they arose. The celebration of the

five-hundredth anniversary of Columbus's arrival in the Americas
has shown how inextricably intertwined were the motives of missionaries and explorers. As one *conquistador*, Bernal Diaz,
expressed it, Europeans went to the New World "to serve God
and His Majesty, to give light to those who were in darkness, and
to grow rich, as all men desire to do." For many, whether among
the colonizers or the colonized, the spread of Christianity and
that of Western civilization appeared to be indistinguishable. As
the famous missionary David Livingstone announced to the students at Cambridge University in 1858, "I go back to Africa to
make an open path for commerce and Christianity."

The inability to distinguish between the two movements led
to other attitudes, such as racial superiority. The Industrial Revolution in the West gave increasing technological power to the
colonizing nations. Missionaries were courted by the peoples to
whom they went because of the tools and machines they possessed and the literacy needed to operate them. As Stephen Neill
pointed out, in 1818 the King of Madagascar was more interested
in the ability of David Jones of the London Missionary Society
to bring in bricklayers, ironworkers, and a printing press than
he was in the Christianity they professed. When Christianity
seemed to be attracting attention, the regime began a violent
persecution and all evangelism in the country was halted for a
generation.

All missionaries, whether they wanted it or not, had behind
them the armed might of the industrialized nations. In China,
for instance, permission for missionaries to proceed into the
interior to carry on their work was written into a series of "une-
qual treaties" which were forced on the country following its
defeat in wars between 1842 and 1900. The rising standard of
living in the West which resulted from a combination of technology with capitalist financial accumulation came to be inter-
preted by all Europeans—including missionaries—as
"civilization." This quality, somehow associated with the spiritual
blessings of the gospel, made them feel superior to the "heathen" cultures they encountered.

How this superiority manifested itself in missionary practice
began to become evident toward the end of the nineteenth cen-

tury. For example, when the first African bishop, Samuel Adjai Crowther, died in 1891, the missionaries in the field opposed the election of another African. An earlier generation had seen nothing but gain in the choice of an indigenous leader as distinguished as Crowther. But a younger generation, accustomed to the "blessings" of what we would today call a more developed society, argued that no African was as yet equal in Christian nurture to a European.

A further example will show that the above incident was not isolated. The Japanese convert Uchimura Kanzo had at first accepted the belief that Western culture was superior because it was Christian. But when he visited the United States he was dismayed to find there not the kingdom of God but much corruption, and people who looked down on him for his differently coloured skin.

In his autobiographical essay, *How I Became a Christian*, he wrote,

> In no other respect, however, did Christendom appear to me more like heathendom than in a strong race prejudice still existing among its people. After a "century of dishonour," the copper-colored children of the forest from whom the land was wrested by many a cruel and inhuman means, are still looked upon by the commonalty as no better than buffaloes or Rocky Mountain sheep, to be trapped and hunted like wild beasts.

After going on to describe the treatment of black people, he continued,

> But strong and unchristian as their feeling is against the Indians and the Africans, the prejudice, the aversion, the repugnance, which they entertain against the children of Sina [China] are something which we in heathendom have never seen the like.

And of course, no one could distinguish between those Chinese and the Japanese Uchimura, so he himself experienced many indignities during his stay in that "Christian" land.

Today the commercial and colonial empires are breaking up

following half a century of political and economic upheaval which has led to two world wars and innumerable local conflicts. The struggles for freedom and independence on the part of those nations once dominated by the West have placed the churches in what we now call the Third World in a position that is, to say the least, ambiguous, and have called our accepted assumptions about mission into question. The contradiction between the liberating message of the gospel and the actual position of indigenous Christians, as members of churches which represent institutional extensions of Western society, has placed many in a situation of conflict that has become almost intolerable for them. Many places have responded by founding independent, sectarian churches. In the case of one nation, China, this clash has resulted in the total disappearance of the traditional denominational structure of Protestantism, and a situation close to schism for Roman Catholics. Even in those countries where some institutional connection remains, leaders who were once obedient servants of a Western-style enterprise now deny customs or structures which appear to them to be relics of colonial days. And the contradictions are not allayed by the continued bondage to the great international, commercial conglomerates in which third-world societies find themselves.

The contradictions between preaching and practice become painfully clear when we survey the world as it exists after five hundred years of Western, Christian missionary activity. Where we preached salvation (liberation), we have brought colonial and economic oppression. Even though a measure of political autonomy may have been achieved by many of the states of Africa and Asia, the gap in standard of living between those nations and the affluent countries of Europe and America continues to grow. Where we preached peace, a crescendo of warfare has ensued. The conflicts raging in Angola, Somalia, and the Soudan; the continued activity of right-wing death squads in Central America (and many other places) can all be related to the aftermath of the colonial era.

We have extolled the blessedness of the poor while we increasingly profited and grew rich at their expense. Trade practices which turned third-world countries like the Philippines or Brazil into supply areas for the affluent North; fiscal policies in our own country which have increased unemployment: all these have led to a growing gap between rich and poor. Where we promised that in Christ there would be no difference of race or class, we have raised up whole states such as South Africa, or situations such as those in which our own native people find themselves, founded on racial discrimination and domination of the many by the privileged few. As Christians we stood by and washed our hands of the excesses of imperialism, but we did not reject the riches which accrued as a result. As Helmut Gollwitzer has pointed out, it is that part of the world which we have called heathen that stands today in the place of the poor man, Lazarus, whom God took to Abraham's bosom, while the Christian nations look like the rich man whom Jesus said God condemned to everlasting fire (Luke 16:23).

In this context, a chorus of voices from the Third World is forcing us as Christians to rethink the assumptions about mission that we have been calling traditional. The truth of each one of the basic principles we have summarized has been questioned and found wanting.

1.   Our emphasis on the Great Commission as an imperative for mission has allowed us to stress what we do to others, making the communication of the gospel seem like a one-way process. *We* became the bearers of truth to the ignorant heathen. A young Baptist pastor from West Africa described in one of my classes how his people were taught to despise their own way of life. "The missionaries behaved," he said, "as if only they knew God's will. Throughout our centuries of history it was as if God had completely neglected us."

Yet many other aspects of Christ's teaching reveal a quite different, more reciprocal, or two-way approach. When people came to Jesus for help, his first words to them were often in the form of a question, "What do *you* think?" (e.g., Mark 9:21, 10:3; Luke 10:26). Jesus used parables to announce the kingdom because their interpretation required participation and response from the hearer (Matthew 13:34).

St. Paul describes Jesus' mission in terms far more compatible with the obscurity it actually endured than the triumphalist assumptions that have characterized so much modern missionary thinking (historical records of the time hardly mention Jesus, allowing some modern critics to doubt whether he actually existed at all). "God sent his Son, born of a woman, born under the law" (Galatians 4:4). "[Christ Jesus] . . . made himself nothing, assuming the nature of a slave" (Philippians 2:7). In contrast to the mighty technological and economic power that has stood behind the modern missionary movement, Jesus constantly identified himself with the powerless "little ones": children (Mark 9:33–37, 10:13–16); women (Mark 14:3–9; Luke 7:36–50; Mark 15:40–41, 16:1–8; Luke 8:1–3); the poor (Luke 6:20, 16:19–31), and social outcasts (Mark 2:15–17; Matthew 21:32).

Incidentally, did the Great Commission actually represent, as Lambeth '88 phrased it, "Jesus' primary command to his disciples"? If it did, why then did those same disciples have such a hard time making up their minds whether or not it would be right to take the gospel to the Gentiles (Acts 11:1–4, 15:1–29; Galatians 2:1–10)? Modern New Testament scholars draw a clear distinction between pre- and post-resurrection sayings of Jesus. In the case of the latter, Christ's actual words and the early church's interpretation have become closely identified. It is not at all clear that the historical Jesus approved of taking the gospel outside the Jewish nation. What about his reply to the Syrophoenician woman (Mark 7:27)? Or Matthew 23:15, "You travel over sea and land to make a single convert [literally, a proselyte]; and you make the new convert twice as much a child of hell as yourselves"? Yet once the leap from Judaism to the Gentiles was made by Peter, Paul, and the others, it became clear that the church was acting in Christ's Spirit (Acts 11:1–18).

2. Over against the "special vocation" assumption, the theology of the New Testament makes clear that *all* who have been made members of Christ in baptism become participators in the divine mission (John 20:21–22; 1 Peter 2:9). As we bear Christ's cross we follow Jesus,

> to bring good news to the poor . . . .
> to proclaim release to the captives

and recovery of sight to the blind,
to let the oppressed go free,
[and] to proclaim the year of Jubilee
(*Luke 4:18-19*).

These words place Jesus in the tradition of the prophets of the Hebrew Scriptures (in the above passage Jesus is quoting from Isaiah 61) who proclaimed God's judgment on the economic and political structures of their day. The reference to the Year of Jubilee comes from Leviticus 25. There all practising Jews were commanded every forty-nine years to pronounce—among other things—a moratorium on debts, in which all slaves would be freed and land lost through debt would be returned to its original owner. In other words, the gap between rich and poor would be abolished. Of course, historically, the facts of life made this command a kind of dream. But Jesus is here saying that in the commonwealth of God which he is bringing, this dream will come true.

So to follow Christ will certainly involve *all* Christians in personal witness and the conversion of individuals. But such witness will also include involvement in the struggles for economic justice and political liberation that are going on today all around us; struggles against racism and poverty and sexism in our own country as well as solidarity with similar movements in Asia, Africa, and Latin America.

3.　Modern insight into the evils of imperialism and the human suffering attendant on the industrial development of the West now make it impossible to accept the former, clear division of the world into Christian and Heathen. We have already read Uchimura Kanzo's criticism of this kind of thinking. In later life he condemned even more fiercely as "false prophets" the leaders of the "Christian" nations when they approved of war and imperial expansion, which they justified in the name of Jesus Christ, the Prince of Peace:

[They] advocate the need for increased arms at the same time as they proclaim themselves servants of Christ; [they] brag of their many friends and plan to spread the Gospel through smooth social graces, and they argue that in this world we must use its ways to build God's kingdom on earth.

Thus, these so-called Christian leaders acted no differently from the leaders of his own militarist, but "heathen," country.

In short, it is a contradiction in terms to call one part of the world Christian and another Heathen. Certainly, all Christians are sent on God's mission. But God is also already present in every part of the world and has been active in creating every culture (John 1:3). Thus, the Christian from the West who goes to another country needs always to be sensitive to what God has already done there, and not try to foist his or her own customs on it, just because they are familiar. Not only are we in the West meant to "help people out there," but we are also to proclaim God's judgment on injustice in our own economic and political institutions which we now see to be oppressing the very people we have been sent to aid.

Nor can we look upon one culture as being more Christian than another, as did our missionary forebears when they dressed the people of Africa or the Pacific Islands in European clothes. That kind of assumption lay behind the practice of making proselytes which both Jesus and Paul rejected (Matthew 23:15; Galatians 3:28). All humanity has been made in God's image (Genesis 1:27). The Spirit blows where he/she wills (John 3:8) and works to redeem *all* cultures. Cultural imperialism is no better than political or economic imperialism.

4.   Accordingly, conversion means the "turning" to God of a person, through the grace of Christ, *within the totality of his/her own culture* (Romans 12:1-2); a change in life which includes external behaviour as well as internal transformation. Conversion is the opposite of proselytism, which seeks to take persons *out of* their own culture and implant them into ours. Conversion is the beginning of a process of growth through which God works to redeem all people *within* the culture in which they live, with all the distinctive customs and practices which those cultures have developed through history. Because Christianity in the Third World is beginning to show us what this means today, we are witnessing an exciting, new phenomenon of plurality and abundance of gifts, such as has never existed before in history.

Yet, precisely because this phenomenon is so new, it may become a problem for us in the West. The dismay displayed by many Western delegates to the 1991 Canberra Assembly of the World Council of Churches at the apparent "syncretism" of a theological presentation by the Korean, woman theologian Chung Hyun Kyung illustrates this problem. For centuries we have been accustomed to understand our form of Christianity as absolute and normative. So it shocks us to find others developing a different interpretation (e.g., of the person of Christ) or worshipping in different ways (dancing during a service in Africa or Korea; letting off firecrackers at the eucharist in the Philippines!). But, as the Chinese theologian C. S. Song has written, if we believe in a Christ through whom *all* things were made (John 1:3), we can no longer say that only the Western form is normative. Thus, "Christians don't have to pose as saviours of the whole world. . . . It's God working through us Christians and also *God working through other people as well*" (the italics are mine). This view of the contribution to Christianity made by non-Western cultures is shared by other third-world theologians such as K. H. Ting in China and Raimundo Panikkar in India.

Consequently, articles of belief such as the creeds, once seen as basic statements, relevant for all people in every age, will now have to be understood as products of a certain culture and time. Phrases such as "of one substance with the Father" or "three persons and one God" have come from a Greek philosophy of the fourth century, unintelligible today to the people of Africa or Asia, not to mention our own young people. So our creeds may have to be changed in the light of new cultural contacts. Indeed, it is impossible to see how radically new insights about cultures will change our approach to belief. Are Christianity and the gospel one and the same thing? Or is Christianity a cultural product of the West, as Buddhism or Confucianism are of the East? Has not God been revealed in these faiths as well?

Moreover, our respect for faiths and cultures in other lands will compel us to look with new eyes at other faiths and cultures in our own land. A few years ago, a scandal arose when those responsible for the Women's Day of Prayer consulted North American native women in the preparation of a form of service for that day. Expressions such as "Great Spirit" and "Mother Earth" seemed to many like pagan accretions, alien to Christianity, so some Anglican bishops banned the use of the form of service in their dioceses. Today, such friendly consultation has become a matter of course, so that Christians acknowledge native spirituality as something valuable in its own right.

To return to our theme, conversion for those who live in a Western society can mean a growth in "holy and creative nonconformity" (Romans 12:2); an increasing expansion of our understanding of God's demand (to love God, and our neighbour as ourself), as contrasted with the demands of the culture in which we live (consumerism, aggressive competition, anti-social individualism, exploitation of class, race, or sex, etc.).

No wonder, then, that Christians face a crisis in their faith and activity concerning mission. We are being compelled to rethink almost everything we have learned—a painful task indeed. Love of, and loyalty to, our leader Jesus Christ remain the same, but the paths along which Christ is leading us have become challenging, new ones.

Yet we do not need to see this period of change in entirely negative terms. Crises can be positive experiences as well. The word *crisis* comes from a Greek verb which means 'to judge'. As David Paton wrote thirty-five years ago in a little book about the Christian experience of the Chinese revolution, God has judged the missionary movement and found it wanting. But the Greek word can also mean 'to choose' or 'to discern'(the English word *discriminate* comes directly from that Greek word). In Japan and other East Asian countries the word for crisis is written with two Chinese characters, one of which means 'danger' (negative) and the other 'opportunity' (positive). Theologians in the Third World see this opportunity to choose as a unique and demanding *kairos*, a Greek word which denotes a moment in time when God calls the people to decide between two ways, one of life and one of death. So then, a crisis can be a chance for a new start, an opportunity to discern where God is leading us.

For Discussion

1. How does the change in thinking about mission affect you, personally?

2. What does it mean to you when we say that we no longer understand the Great Commission to be "Jesus' primary command to his disciples"?
    Why do you think that people are not volunteering to go overseas as missionaries today?

3. If we see a time of crisis as (a) danger and (b) opportunity, what would we say are the dangerous things in our own Christian life, and where does opportunity lie?

4. What are the positive aspects of mission for a Christian today?

5. What contribution do you think Christians from the Third World can make to us here in Canada?

For Further Reading

Roland Allen, *Missionary Methods, Saint Paul's or Ours?* (London: World Dominion Press, 1930).

David B. Barrett, ed., *World Christian Encyclopedia* (Nairobi and London: Oxford University Press, 1982).

William Carey, *An Enquiry into the Obligation of Christians to Use Means for the Conversion of the Heathen* (Facsimile of 1792 edition, London: Carey Kingsgate Press, 1961).

Anthony J. Gittins, *Bread for the Journey: The Mission of Transformation and the Transformation of Mission* (Maryknoll, NY: Orbis Books, 1993).

Helmut Gollwitzer, *The Rich Christians and Poor Lazarus* (New York: Macmillan, 1970).

Chung Hyun Kyung, *Struggle to Be the Sun Again: Introducing Asian Women's Theology* (Maryknoll, NY: Orbis Books, 1990).

Jose Miguez-Bonino, "The Present Crisis in Mission," in G. H. Anderson and T. E. Stransky, ed., *Mission Trends No. 1* (New York: New Paulist Press, 1974).

David Paton, *Christian Missions and the Judgment of God* (London: SCM Press, 1953).

2 The World We Live In

When one is lost, the common-sense thing to do is, first, to stop and look around to get some idea of where one is. After that, one may ask someone the way, or consult a map. If we Christians admit that we are feeling lost today, the first thing we can do is look around and see where we are: just what the context of our lives looks like. Are we some place where we want to be? If not, can we find some landmarks that will guide us to where we want to go? To pick out three of the most obvious landmarks, we see that we live, firstly, in a world of change; secondly, in a world of science and technology; and, thirdly, in a revolutionary world. Let us examine each one of these landmarks more closely.

A World of Change

Change is a fundamental aspect of human life. We are born, we grow up, we grow old, we die. And the environment in which we live shows the same constant change: the sun stands still only in fairy tales. But the way we *notice* change is more complicated. We may take the cycle of life for granted if we can rest assured of unchanging powers supporting us. "Change and decay in all around I see," wrote the Victorian poet. "O thou who changest not, abide with me." Until fairly recently, we believed that tradition—the way it has always been done—derived its authority from God's unchanging nature so that, in the midst of change, we could stand fast, supported by "the eternal verities."

The problem is that in certain ages, and particularly in this day and age, society changes so rapidly that even the eternal verities appear to be threatened. God seems to have deserted us. "Awake, Lord! Why are you sleeping?" cries the psalmist, echoing a desperation all of us must have felt at some time or other. Ever since the Industrial Revolution (that word *revolution* itself stands for uncontrollably rapid change!) things have been changing so fast that even God seems to have lost control. In our own day, the sixties represented a time of particularly uncontrollable change, expressions such as "future shock" and "death of God" reflected the near panic that people felt. And even today the pace does not seem to have slowed down much.

The information revolution is just one example of this rapid change. Those of us who grew up before World War II were accustomed to depend on two main sources for storing and finding information: our memories and books (libraries). But today, with the assistance of computers, the gathering, storing, classification, and recovery of information can be done in what seems to us oldsters to be a miraculously short and efficient way. One has only to master the intricacies of operating the machine. For those who have grown up more recently, it all seems matter of fact, but the use of computers to assist in thinking remains a basic change with which many of us have problems. We feel lost and scared: out of control.

Now there are at least two ways that we can deal with change. One is to act like the proverbial ostrich: bury our heads in the sand and pretend that nothing is happening. Not only Christians but also members of other faiths have chosen this way. The growth of fundamentalism in North America and elsewhere reflects the reaction of those who try to take refuge from change in an authoritarian religion which stresses the unchanging nature of belief and practice. Although not so extreme as fundamentalism, such conservative causes as the Renewal Fellowship in the United Church, or the Prayer Book Society and the Anglican Catholic Church of North America in the Anglican Church of Canada reveal the unease felt by so many at changes in the language used in worship or at practices such as the ordination of women and homosexuals. But such Christians need to remind themselves about St. Paul's description of

> Christ Jesus,
> who, though in the form of God,
>   did not regard equality with God

as something to be exploited,
but emptied himself,
 taking the form of a slave,
 and living a human life.
(*Philippians 2:6-7*)

So Christians who respond to change by trying to act as if it did not happen show that they have forgotten their vow to follow a Person who has embraced human life with all the changes and chances that that involves.

Christ's birth, life, death, and resurrection provide us with a model of salvation (liberation): not by running away from, but by becoming involved in and grappling with change. "Look! I am making everything new!" says God in St. John's heavenly vision (Revelation 21:5). In baptism we have been born again into a new society, becoming part of Christ's resurrection body, in which God has changed us and raised us up to a new beginning after our death to sin (Colossians 2:12-13). Thus our life as Christians is itself interwoven with change. The Holy Spirit blows, like the wind, wherever he/she wills, and we are given the courage to follow.

If we identify ourselves with this Christ who was "obedient to the Law" (i.e., to the fabric of human existence which involves constant change), we shall view the way that the faith has been passed on to us (tradition) with freshly opened eyes. No longer shall we be able to accept a kind of static definition of tradition —that which has been believed "everywhere, always, and by everyone"—but we shall come to think of ourselves as little fishes, swimming in a great river. From time to time this river has been enlarged by tributaries, bringing in fresh water. St. Paul shocked the first-generation church by proposing that Gentiles might become Christians without first accepting circumcision. This was something that had never been explicitly mentioned in the gospel, though admittedly implied in Jesus' life and teaching.

Three hundred years later, St. Athanasius and others introduced ways of describing Christ's nature that were just as new to the biblical tradition as St. Paul's had been. The New Testament had never come to grips with what it meant, exactly, to say that Jesus was God's child. This problem led to much controversy and was eventually answered by saying that Christ was both human and divine, "of one substance with the Father." Because this definition appeared to contradict the biblical teaching that there is only one God, many people objected. Yet in time, though not without opposition and even violent struggle, the doctrine was accepted and has become part of our universal tradition, enshrined in the creeds. And the church's history is littered with many similar cases.

One example closer to our own day, and very relevant to the theme of mission, relates to the change that has taken place in our understanding of the eucharistic liturgy. As late as the last century in the Anglican Communion, the eucharist was celebrated infrequently and, in common with other denominations' communions, was understood principally as an act of private devotion. But the Liturgical Movement, which began about a hundred years ago, recalled Christians to the practice of the early church, where the eucharist represented the corporate offering of the People of God assembled for their weekly worship. Historic works such as Dom Gregory Dix's *The Shape of the Liturgy*, or Father Hastings Smyth's *Discerning the Lord's Body*, also taught people about the intrinsic relation between worship in the liturgy and action for social justice in society.

These changes did not take place without conflict and opposition. Priests went to prison for putting candles on the altar and wearing vestments. And that opposition to change has not ended in our own day. Congregations still exist where Morning Prayer according to the 1959 *Book of Common Prayer* represents the standard service. But a weekly celebration of the eucharist according to the *Book of Alternative Services* has become much more widespread. Its language is now the English that all of us speak, rather than an imitation of how people talked four hundred years ago. Its call to mission at the end—"Go forth in the name of Christ"—now reminds us that God sends each one of us into the world as witnesses for Christ.

So we need not be surprised if change should continue to crop up (e.g., the ordination of gays and women, female imagery about God). We need only to be assured that the changes do not run contrary to the mainstream. Does what is being proposed deepen and widen our understanding of Christ's teaching and example? Is it more loving? That process of discernment may take a while, even generations, to work itself out. But we need to take risks, as Jesus did when he challenged "orthodox" interpretations of the Law (his own tradition). When he taught (Matthew 5:21), "You have heard that it was said to those of ancient times [i.e., traditionally] . . . But I say to you," he threatened the leaders of his community who saw their duty to be one of a strict guarding of the tradition. And it was this clash that eventually led to Jesus' death. Today, in the case of woman priests, such statements as those contained in Genesis 1:27 or Galatians 3:28 push us to review the tradition and to strive for greater equality in both church and society. That this striving may lead to conflict and disagreement for a while cannot deter us. We live in a world of change.

A World of Science and Technology

Science and technology have become such a fundamental part of our lives today that it is difficult to imagine a world without doctors or engineers, airplanes or computers, skyscrapers or factories. The age of technology has meant for all humanity a world of untold blessings: the possibility of increased production; enough to eat with freedom from the threat of famine, flood, or pestilence. Once terrifying scourges like the plague, smallpox, or tuberculosis have become for all practical purposes things of the past. In a high-tech society such as Japan's average life expectancy has increased in the short span of forty years from 43 to 77, a truly incredible leap, with implications that take time to grasp. And, as we all know, these technological changes are interrelated to a constant process of research and experiment in countless scientific laboratories all over the world. The emergence of the scientific method of observation, abstraction, investigation, and generalization has formed the basis of all sorts of other new ways we think in a modern society.

To give only one example, with science and technology has

come a new approach to social change. Before the eighteenth century, social order was regarded as something ordained by God, immutable and sacred. St. Paul, writing to the Christians in Rome, asserted, "The existing authorities have been instituted by God. Therefore whoever resists authority resists what God has appointed and those who resist will incur judgment" (Romans 13:1-2). For St. Paul and for centuries of Christians after him, the authority structures of society—kings, classes, even fathers of families— were part of the original order created by God (like species among animals or strata in rocks) and all we could do was accept them, even though we might not like them or understand their purpose.

But in our day all that has changed. The twin, great revolutions of the eighteenth century (industrial and political) led to a growing understanding of change, and the ability on the part of human beings, through the social sciences, consciously to initiate change and restructuring in the social order. Though such human efforts may be far from error-free, we can still carry out projects for social betterment, whether on a large scale or in more limited ways, the likes of which our ancestors never dreamed. China's recent liberation, so vast and far-reaching despite its discouraging ups and downs, represents only one of the most outstanding examples of such planned change. To many of us the Chinese leadership seems to be going astray these days in their disregard of human rights and the abandonment of co-operative models of development. Nevertheless, the basic change accomplished by the original revolution cannot be denied. And we take for granted every day myriad smaller schemes for social transformation, whether it be the plan for a local housing development or better health care in a developing country.

Both technological and social revolutions have resulted in a basic change in the human approach to knowledge, represented by the emergence of empirical, or experiential, reasoning. Where tradition and authority once reigned, experiment and questioning have become the starting-point for generalization and hypothesis. Where truth was once seen as ontological, or absolute, it now frequently appears as a process in which old understanding, called into doubt by new data, gives place to new theory.

In the realm of religious thought, the most traditional of all human activity, this change in method has posed problems and given rise to anxiety and conservative reaction on the one hand, and outright rejection of belief on the other. New theologies of experience, context, and process, whose method is based on the scientific approach, appear to challenge categories such as miracle or revelation. Such an approach does not contradict the spirit of our faith—no matter what its conservative critics may say—because, in its denial of tradition and authority as absolute, in its assertion that such absolute thinking comes close to superstition or idolatry, scientific thinking was born as a natural outcome of the Christian world-view. In both Hebrew and Christian Scriptures only God is absolute: all else is subject to change and limitation. The Incarnation of God's only Child, "born of a woman, born under the Law," teaches us that the Creator is revealed, not by some mechanical interruption of the cosmos, but through and within its working. Thus, the investigation of the universe, of human history, or of society, represents tasks for the theologian just as much as for the natural or social scientist.

Indeed, theology has a contribution to make beyond the realm of what we may call purely scientific thought. The latter must, by its nature, limit itself to data that can be measured and, in some sense, controlled. It must isolate and abstract its data in order to study it, thus natural and social scientists always deal with a reality that is partial. Theologians deal with that part of human existence which is much more difficult to measure but without which the material aspects of life lose their significance: that which concerns the ultimate values and goals by which human beings shape their lives, by which the rest of life achieves meaning and purpose. Philosophy, which mediates between the physical and social sciences and theology, provides us with the language and concepts by which we can investigate the spiritual realm. But it is the Christian conviction that only in the contemplation and worship of God can we find the true purpose of the universe (Psalm 111.10, 2 Corinthians 5.14–17). So theology attempts to describe for us something that is ultimately indescribable, but without which, nevertheless, we cannot live without attempting in some way to understand.

It is this contemplation of a realm which stretches beyond us that makes us pause and consider that technology can confront humanity not as a blessing but as a curse. For the first time in history, machines present us with the possibility of leisure and time to think and pray, available in past generations only to the wealthy elites of a given society. Yet the same leisure which frees can also mean slavery if it comes in the form of unemployment. A multitude of critics of technological society, beginning with William Blake, F. D. Maurice, and Karl Marx, and continuing in our own day with Jacques Ellul and George Grant, right down to Ursula Franklin in her Massey Lectures, has reminded us of this ambiguity.

To begin at the most obvious level, there is the tendency in a technological society to judge all reality and value in terms of measurable quantity or functional efficiency. How well does a machine work? may be a natural question for an engineer to ask, but a more complex one when society or an individual is being measured. We can gain some understanding with figures and statistics of concrete phenomena, but can we see or touch a soul? Thus we often have the experience of seeing a factory, or a school, or hospital in a certain area closed down, not because the people there no longer need it, but because it is not showing a profit, or because someone has decided that too few people live around the area to make continuing operation efficient. Or societies may be adjudged good or bad by the rise or fall of the GNP, not by the quality of life shared by all its citizens.

The tendency to judge the whole of life on the basis of the way one part works or, to put it another way, to look at the way human beings live and think as if they were machines, we call *reductionism*. This kind of thinking is not limited to the mechanical model. Technological society likes to divide every area of human life into specialized compartments—economics, politics, art, medicine, psychology, religion, and so forth—each part being seen as playing a function, but not necessarily related. The claim to be a basic or most important factor on the part of any one of these areas is reductionist because it *reduces* the way we think about the whole of life to the method and material used for one part.

Thus it is reductionist thinking to claim, as we so often hear, that unemployment is unavoidable if we are to combat inflation (in other words, the cause of social dislocation is *nothing but* economic). The opposite of reductionist thinking is holistic thinking, which insists on taking human existence as a whole. Each field of learning can contribute to a total understanding of life, but only disaster can ensue if one area claims absolute pre-eminence.

A third level at which science and technology can bring a curse on humanity, and not a blessing, emerges out of their historical relation to capitalism. The technological and bourgeois revolutions, it is generally agreed, developed in Western Europe side by side, although the exact connection between the two is unclear. Technology developed with advances in agriculture and navigation, at first slowly, by trial and error, then more rapidly as it was seen to be a profitable enterprise. Its evolution was aided by the parallel emergence about six hundred years ago of city merchants (the bourgeoisie) as dominant actors in building a new social order based on trade and finance. The growth of capital and industry (the partnership between merchants and technology) resulted in greater affluence for more people than feudalism had been able to supply. With this affluence there developed greater freedom and more broadly based forms of government such as democracy.

But the fact remains that capitalism has contributed a rather sinister bias to technology. Over the past three hundred years, alongside democratic government, a society has developed in which financial and productive power came to be concentrated in the hands of a relatively few people. This power increased exponentially as newer machines and techniques were invented. Consequently, the majority of people found themselves virtually shut out from the ability to make significant decisions about matters that affected their own destinies. Where they would live; what kind of work they would choose; even what they would eat or wear: all these and many more choices and decisions were strictly limited for most people. All most of us can do today is to buy what someone else has decided to stock in the supermarket or department store.

Of course, the peasants in the Middle Ages possessed even less power of choice. Where they would live or what they would do depended largely on where they were born. But that was seen as something that God had ordained and one could look forward to freedom and happiness in the life to come in heaven. In the new society, political democracy made choice at one level—the vote—possible, while the growth of the social sciences offered the prospect of deliberate structural change. Thus the feeling that one might be shut out from participation in this and other areas of choice became even more intolerable. Even farmers, who live closest to the productive power of the earth, are not free to grow what they want for themselves. They find that what is to be grown on the farm is now decided by someone else, whether it is a bank, a food conglomerate, or some impersonal market demand. So, in order to survive, they have to grow what they are told to and buy what they would formerly have grown.

To sum up, we find ourselves living in a world where a relative few possess enormous wealth and, therefore, the economic and political power to decide how the technology shall be operated. The rest of us, though many may be able to live quite comfortably, find ourselves excluded from all but token control over our own lives. The more affluent a capitalist society becomes, the greater is the number of the middle-income group, or middle class as it may be called. But even in such societies (as we are learning today), unemployment lurks around the corner and abject poverty continues to exist. And in most countries of the West the working class, though it may enjoy a relatively high income, never knows whether its members will have a job tomorrow or not.

For Christians, a world of economic inequality means a world in which hate reigns, not love (1 John 3:13–17). All human beings have been made in God's image, to share in the divine activity of creation. That a few people should try to monopolize that right, while the majority find themselves excluded, goes against God's will (Jeremiah 22:13–17).

A Revolutionary World

So great has the concentration of power to control the ownership and use of technology become that economic inequality now extends into the international sphere. For over a generation, statesmen and scholars have been pointing to the radical division in the world between rich and poor nations. You may have noticed the term "Third World" appearing from time to time in the preceding pages as a description of that part of the world whose economy is often described as "developing" in contrast to the more affluent, or "developed," societies of the northern hemisphere.

Some may feel that this term is a put-down, equivalent to expressions like "uncivilized" or "heathen." Why should some nations be labeled as belonging to a "third world," implying that they are inferior to those who live in the "second" or "first" worlds? For that reason some writers prefer to use different expressions such as "two-thirds world," or "north-south" in order to distinguish the rich and poor areas of the world. But the term "Third World" is not used here in any pejorative sense but as a technical term to describe a situation of economic dependence and oppression that has developed over a period of time and as a result of certain historical forces. It was first used by representatives of those societies themselves as a shorthand way of describing an injustice, in order to distance themselves from the "developed" capitalist and socialist nations of the northern hemisphere. One recent Japanese scholar has described the difference as follows:

> The population of the Third World represents 52% of the total population of the world. But in terms of its Gross National Product (GNP) it represents barely 18% of the world's total. In contrast to that, the GNP of the advanced capitalist countries, whose population amounts to a mere 17% of the total, accounts for 62% of the total world GNP.

Such inequality, as we shall see if we study its origins scientifically, did not come about by chance. It is the end result, first of the colonialism of the nineteeenth century, and now of a system of trade created by those who hold the power to control technology. The wealth of the affluent nations, such as the U.S.A., Western Europe, Canada, or Japan, depends on the existence of areas of poverty which can supply raw materials and labour at low cost; at the same time loans made to those areas in the name of development increase their dependency. The inequality resulting from this system seems to be growing, rather than diminishing. So we can only conclude that the intolerable suffering we see today in such countries as Bangladesh, Ethiopia, or sub-Saharan Africa represents an aspect of a world system created by capitalism and backed up by science and technology.

True, local features such as tribal rivalry (Eritrea, Somalia) and natural disasters (floods in Bangladesh, drought in Africa) have exacerbated the situation. But the histories of other nations, including our own, show that economic development can provide a base for the creation of infrastructure and the elimination of local rivalry. The terrible truth is that this situation has occurred at the very moment in history that science and technology have provided the world with the knowledge and means to abolish hunger and disease everywhere. Is there no other way to maintain our own high standard of living? The emergence of former third-world nations such as South Korea, Taiwan, and Singapore as economic powers presents a threat to the stability of our way of life, evident to anyone in the rivalry between Asia and North America for car sales.

So then, it is no wonder that the people of the Third World should attempt, by violence if necessary, to free themselves from the vicious circle of debt and poverty which has resulted from the transnational concentration of power. Everywhere we look today we can see the revolutionary process going on. While these words are being written, South Africa occupies the front line of the drive towards liberation. Moreover, the sympathy expressed by many third-world countries for Iraq in the Persian Gulf conflict reflects another facet of the struggle between rich and poor nations.

In some countries the drive toward liberation has achieved a measure of success, but more often it has been quenched by the establishment of what are known as "technocratic security states." In country after country, oppressive regimes, backed up by the high technology of the advanced nations, maintain the power of a wealthy minority against the poverty of the majority. This power is maintained through the media of communications, computers, nuclear power, and weaponry that once existed only in science fiction, not to mention horribly sophisticated methods of torture, all of which demonstrate the perversion of a God-given blessing. Incredible sums of money are diverted to this devilish production, designed only to maintain the monopoly of the rich.

In a few countries—Japan, the U.S.A., England, Canada, Australia, Western Europe, and so forth—relative affluence allows a certain degree of political freedom. Yet in terms of real human freedom, the power to make decisions about one's own life, we find ourselves, like Esau, having sold our birthright for a pot of stew (Genesis 25.29–34). We are able to maintain our affluence *because* we acquiesce in a system which, in countless places such as South Africa, the Philippines. South Korea, Indonesia, Guatemala, maintains inequality by means of the technocratic security state.

Even among the affluent nations, developments hint that any real threat to the reigning power structure could bring on a similar situation. Anyone over forty can remember how Prime Minister Trudeau invoked the War Measures Act against the people of Quebec in 1973. And the way in which our native people were treated at Oka in August 1992 is still fresh in our minds. Outside Canada, the deliberations of high level bodies, such as the Group of Seven Summit or the International Monetary Fund (on both of which representatives of our country sit), demonstrate the direct relationships that exist between the interests of investors in the affluent nations and repression in the Third World.

This kind of heartless action can exist because technology creates a frame of mind which thinks, not in terms of living beings, but of machines and figures in account books. We have even deluded ourselves into believing that this mechanical model reveals how the universe functions. As we so often hear our leaders intoning, we may not like the disregard of human rights that goes on in third-world countries, but we are forced to accept "the laws of the market place'' which so often make it necessary. This exclusive emphasis on the necessity of a free play of market forces, without state interference, is often called *monetarism* and was in great vogue during the Thatcher-Reagan-Mulroney years. We may be moving away from it in some ways, yet it often reveals itself in the thinking of conservative economists and bankers.

For the Christian, though, it is not the market but God who rules the universe. The monetarist myth is nothing but a hoax to blind us to the inordinate concentration of power that wealth and technology have reinforced in a capitalist society. Thus, for Christians the drive for liberation, whether in the Third World, or among native people and women in our own land, or on the part of any oppressed minority, people, or class, becomes something significantly theological, analogous to the liberation of the Children of Israel from Egypt.

All the communications media, whether through consumer-oriented advertising, or by their filtering of the information available to us, are dedicated to shaping the minds of the majority in the direction of the materialist myth. By this skilful manipulation of the climate of thought which surrounds us—from what was really going on during the Gulf War to what model of car to buy—we in the affluent countries are kept docile and uncritical, subservient to the interests of those who seek their own profit rather than the common good. In truth these are the ''principalities and powers in high places'' (Ephesians 6:12) against which the Christian struggles in our day.

For Discussion

1. How does your life differ from that of your parents because of changes in technology?

2. How do you deal with change in your life: e.g., moving from one place or country to another; changes at work; change in church?

3. Does the word *revolution* necessarily denote violence? What about such uses as Industrial Revolution, Information Revolution, etc.?

4. How can we use modern technology in a positive way (to the glory of God)?

5. What does theology mean for you? Is it just another specialized (academic, boring) discipline? Or is it the way Christians can reflect on their faith in relation to their experience in everyday life?

For Further Reading

John B. Cobb & D. R. Griffin, *Process Theology* (Philadelphia: Westminster Press, 1976). [On change and theology]

Ursula Franklin, *The Real World of Technology* (The Massey Lectures, Montreal & Toronto, CBC Enterprises, 1990).

E. J. Hobsbawm, *The Age of Revolution* (New York & Toronto, Mentor Books, 1962).

Michael Ingham, *Rites for a New Age* (Toronto: Anglican Book Centre, 1986).

Brewster Kneen, *From Land to Mouth: Understanding the Food System*, second helping (Toronto: SC Press, 1993).

L. S. Stavrianos, *Global Rift: The Third World Comes of Age* (New York: William Morrow, 1981).

Alvin Toffler, *Future Shock* (New York: Bantam Books, 1971).

3 Calling and Sending in the Bible

In every period in history when Christians have faced new conditions, they have looked back to the sources of their tradition for new directions. When William Carey became conscious of the need to arouse the Protestant Christians of England to God's call for work overseas—a call dimly heard since the Reformation— he turned to the Great Commission for a direction which would apply to the context of his time. Today, new times demand new directions, so we are driven once more to examine our sources; to discover, if possible, what God is saying to us within the context of our time.

Perhaps our first reaction to such a suggestion will be a sense of powerlessness. Is there *anything* we can do? The odds seem so tremendous, the channels of action so limited, our allies so few. Christians who seek in real earnest for a new direction are a tiny minority. The majority seems to be satisfied with the illusion that happiness consists in owning a house of one's own, a car or two or three, a cottage at the lake, or a boat. Even the leadership of our churches, by and large, appears more concerned with matters of institutional self-preservation than with mission or prophetic witness. Those sections of Christianity which emphasize security and extrication from the problems of society seem to be growing rapidly, while churches which advocate involvement in change seem to fade inexorably away.

Yet for God's chosen to be a remnant—a struggling minority—is nothing new. The later prophets of Israel saw their nation coming to such a state. The early church faced an even more critical situation. "Think what sort of people you are, whom God has called," writes St. Paul. "Not many of you were wise by human standards, not many were powerful, not many were of noble birth. But God chose what is foolish . . . what is weak . . . mere nothings, to overthrow the existing order" (1 Corinthians 1:26–28). The odds then were equally tremendous.

The early church seemed be struggling "not against enemies of flesh and blood, but against the rulers, against the authorities, against the cosmic powers of this present darkness" (Ephesians 6:12). Even when the mighty Roman Empire finally gave in and recognized the Christian movement, historians have estimated that Christians made up only about ten per cent of the total population. This is less than half the number in South Korea today, where about twenty-five per cent are Christian, but where factors such as the unhappy divisions introduced from the West have weakened their power to influence the society.

So then, weakness in numbers or in political power need never be a hindrance to action. After all, in a faith which reveres an obscure young woman as Mother of God and begins one of its gospels with stories of the conception of Elizabeth and the Annunciation to Mary, the theme of powerlessness must be accepted as central. If we examine three representative stories in which leading figures in the Bible are called and sent on a mission, some interesting implications about the connection between powerlessness and mission emerge. Other accounts of God calling people— Hannah, Isaiah, Jonah, Paul of Tarsus—exhibit a similar structure, so we can safely assume that powerlessness is understood in the tradition to be a fundamental aspect of Christian mission. God is the one who "has cast down the powerful from their thrones, and lifted up the lowly." Let us read on and see what other valuable insights emerge.

God Calls Moses

After a long time the king of Egypt died. The Israelites groaned under their slavery, and cried out. Out of the slavery their cry for help rose up to God. God heard their groaning, and God remembered his covenant with Abraham, Isaac, and Jacob. God looked upon the Israelites, and God took notice of them. Moses was keeping the flock of his father-in-law Jethro, the priest of Midian; he led his flock beyond the wilderness and came to Horeb, the mountain of God. There the angel of the Lord appeared to him in a flame of fire out of a bush; he looked, and the bush was blazing, yet it was not consumed. Then Moses said, "I must turn aside and look at this great sight, and see why the bush is not burned up.'' When the Lord saw that he had turned aside to see, God called to him out of the bush, ''Moses, Moses!'' And he said, ''Here I am.'' Then he said, ''Come no closer! Remove the sandals from your feet, for the place on which you are standing is holy ground.'' He said further, ''I am the God of your father, the God of Abraham, the God of Isaac, and the God of Jacob.'' And Moses hid his face, for he was afraid to look at God. Then the Lord said, ''I have observed the misery of my people who are in Egypt; I have heard their cry on account of their taskmasters. Indeed, I know their sufferings, and I have come down to deliver them from the Egyptians, and to bring them up out of that land to a good and broad land, a land flowing with milk and honey, to the country of the Canaanites, the Hittites, the Amorites, the Perizzites, the Hivites, and the Jebusites. The cry of the Israelites has now come to me; I have also seen how the Egyptians oppress them. So come, I will send you to Pharaoh to bring my people, the Israelites, out of Egypt.'' But Moses said to God, ''Who am I that I should go to Pharaoh, and bring the Israelites out of Egypt?'' He said, ''I will be with you; and this shall be the sign for you that it is I who sent you: when you have brought the people out of Egypt, you shall worship God on this mountain.''

(Exodus 2:23—3:12)

God Calls Jeremiah

The words of Jeremiah son of Hilkiah, of the priests who were in Anathoth in the land of Benjamin, to whom the word of the Lord came in the days of King Josiah son of Amon of Judah, in the thirteenth year of his reign. It came also in the days of King Jehoiakim son of Josiah of Judah, and until the end of the eleventh year of King Zedekiah son of Josiah of Judah, until the captivity of Jerusalem in the fifth month. Now the word of the Lord came to me saying, ''Before I formed you in the womb I knew you, and before you were born I consecrated you; I appointed you a prophet to the nations.'' Then I said, ''Ah, Lord God! Truly I do not know how to speak, for I am only a boy.'' But the Lord said to me, ''Do not say, 'I am only a boy'; for you shall go to all to whom I send you, and you shall speak whatever I command you. Do not be afraid of them, for I am with you to deliver you, says the Lord.'' Then the Lord put out his hand and touched my mouth; and the Lord said to me, ''Now I have put my words in your mouth. See, today I appoint you over nations and over kingdoms, to pluck up and pull down, to destroy and to overthrow, to build and to plant.''

(Jeremiah 1:1-10)

Jesus Calls Peter

Once while Jesus was standing beside the lake of Gennesaret, and the crowd was pressing in on him to hear the word of God, he saw two boats there at the shore of the lake; the fishermen had gone out of them and were washing their nets. He got into one of the boats, the one belonging to Simon, and asked him to put out a little way from the shore. Then he sat down and taught the crowds from the boat. When he had finished speaking, he said to Simon, ''Put out into the deep water and let down your nets for a catch.'' Simon answered, ''Master, we have worked all night long but have caught nothing. Yet if you say so, I will let down the nets.'' When they had done this, they caught so many fish that their nets were beginning to break. So they signaled their partners in the other boat to come and help them. And they came and filled both boats, so that they began to sink. But when Simon Peter saw it, he fell down at Jesus' knees, saying, ''Go away from me, Lord, for I am a sinful man!'' For he and all who were with him were amazed at the catch of fish that they had taken; and so also were James and John, sons of Zebedee, who were partners with Simon. Then Jesus said to Simon, ''Do not be afraid; from now on you will be catching people.'' When they had brought their boats to shore, they left everything and followed him.

(Luke 5:1-11)

Even a superficial glance at the above accounts will reveal a structure which is common to all three. First, a context is sketched out in which the need is recognized (Exodus 2:23-25;

Jeremiah 1:1–3; Luke 5:1–3). Next, someone is called (Moses in Exodus 3:4–10; Jeremiah in Jeremiah 1:4–5; and Peter in Luke 5:4–7). Thirdly, in each case that person is overwhelmed by a sense of his own inadequacy to perform the task being asked of him (Exodus 3:6b, 11; compare also 4:10; Jeremiah 1:6; Luke 5:8–10). They argue with God to let them off, but God replies, ''Do not be afraid; I am with you'' (Note that in Luke's account of Peter's call, Jesus is playing God's part). Then, finally, God proceeds to spell out the nature of the mission upon which the person is being sent (it is characteristic of the Hebrew tradition, which the Gospels inherited, that mission is always something *particular* and *concrete*: a kind of embassy upon which the person is being sent and for which that person is accountable (Exodus 3:7–10; Jeremiah 1:7–10; Luke 5:10b).

To sum up, in the face of our powerlessness, God does not make impossible demands. Rather, God takes the initiative and supplies the motive power. That is, the individual, group, or people, is called to participate in some concrete movement that God has already initiated in history (i.e., which is already happening and only needs to be pointed out). It is God who acts—it is God's mission —we are called to co-operate. In the Moses story, Yahweh says, ''I have heard the cry of my people: I am with you.'' (And we look back to the story of Moses' unsuccessful attempt to start a rebellion among the Israelites in Exodus 2:11–15. Now God endorses Moses' leadership and promises success in a second attempt.)

For Christians, Jesus has been sent into the world as a kind of personal climax to God's liberating action. He is sent ''at the *kairos*''—the crucial moment—translated in our versions, ''the fulness of time,'' or ''the appointed time.'' By this we understand a *particular* moment in history—''under Pontius Pilate,'' as the creeds express it—also at the *right* moment: when a number of factors have come together to make that appearance most effective. So then, Jesus sums up in person what it means to be *chosen* by God (the words—*messiah* in Hebrew, *Christ* in Greek—mean ''the one who has been anointed'': the characteristic Hebrew way of describing God's choice of a prophet or king) (See 1 Samuel 16:13; Psalm 105:15; Isaiah 42:1, 45:1; Mark 1:11;

John 1:41).

Jesus' messiahship (i.e., the terms of his mission) consists in his powerlessness in human terms ("born of a woman"—an ordinary human being; "under the law"—limited by time and culture; "taking the position of a slave"—at the very bottom of the class scale in his society; and finally, accepting death in the most painful and disgraceful form known to his day). So it is through this kind of mission that we know, as St. Paul expressed it, that "in Christ God was reconciling the world to Godself." And it is in this kind of mission that we Christians are called to participate: "that message of reconciliation has been entrusted to us" (2 Corinthians 5:19).

Let us now try to understand what this mission means in concrete, somewhat less theological, terms. Two general principles emerge from the biblical illustrations cited above.

1.   All the stories have taken on supernatural (legendary) elements in the telling (the bush burns but is not consumed; there is a miraculous catch of fish; and so forth). These are ways in which the narrator of the story makes sure that the hearers will understand that it is God who is acting. But, basically, God is shown to be acting, not through some miraculous intervention in human affairs, but through the seemingly natural movements, great and small, of history. In the Exodus story Moses is called to become the leader, in sociological terms, of a rebellion by the enslaved Hebrew minority against their Egyptian overlords (note that Moses had already demonstrated his leadership qualifications by killing one of the bosses). There is plenty of theological significance in all this, but at its most basic level it begins as a historical occurrence. We need to learn how to discern these movements of history, just as farmers and fisherfolk learn how to foretell the weather (Luke 12:54–56). Having understood how and where God is at work, we can "judge for ourselves" how and where we are being called to co-operate.

2.   The Bible also tells us that God usually acts historically in the interests of those who are weak and oppressed (the powerless, the poor, the "little ones"). In Jeremiah, the prophet is commanded to show how God chooses Judah, a poor and insignificant pawn, caught in the web of power politics among the great Middle Eastern nations such as Egypt and Assyria, to represent the divine plan. Earlier on, God chose prophets in Israel who were often ordinary working people (Amos 7:14) to defend the cause of the poor or oppressed minorities against the rapacity of the rich and powerful ruling classes (1 Kings 21; Isaiah 61:1-3; Jeremiah 22:13-17).

Jesus and his disciples followed in this tradition. The earliest followers all belonged to groups that were marginal (publicans, prostitutes, Zealots) to the established strata of society, or else had deliberately marginalized themselves as Jesus had done ("left all": Luke 5:11; 8:2-4). As the Marys, Peter, Paul, and James and all the early missionaries demonstrate, Christianity began as a movement of poor and dispossessed people. These powerless people struggled, first against the ruling classes of Palestine, and eventually against the combined might of the entire Roman Empire, in its day the greatest political power in the Western world. No wonder that these earliest Christians saw themselves related to the ancient Hebrews who had struggled against Egypt under Moses' leadership (Acts 7:18-43).

So then, one important touchstone for judging where God is at work in history today will be to discover where "monarchs are being dethroned and the poor are being exalted" (Luke 1:52). One important reason why Christianity in our time is so often like salt that has lost its bite is that the church so often finds itself on the side of the rich rather than of the poor. Wherever the opposite is true, as in Central America, or among the blacks of South Africa, we can usually see new life emerging.

Finally, one word of caution about how we use the Bible when we go to it for guidance in dealing with new situations. The Hebrew and Christian Scriptures were never intended to be consulted like a crystal ball or a pack of Tarot cards that will give an automatic oracle that we can follow without any effort on our part. Many people today, battered by rapid change, uncertainty, and the appearance of new, sometimes frightening, situations with which they feel inadequate to deal, are tempted to take refuge in treating the Bible as an infallible guide to action. Those who say Christians need not fear a nuclear holocaust because God will take them to heaven first, or speak of the conflict in the Middle East as a prelude to Armageddon; or others who regard family planning or equal rights for women as forbidden by Scripture, reflect this "magical" use of the Bible.

Careful reading and study will make it perfectly clear that the Bible was never meant to be used in this way. Its books resemble a great string of beads in myriad colours, sizes, and shapes. Each one—and even the materials out of which a single one is constructed—was put together in response to a particular situation. The questions raised relate to the times and conditions which then existed, some of them more than three thousand years ago, and in societies which differed totally from our own. Thus, because women were subordinated in the patriarchal society of the day, or rich people kept slaves, or St. Paul said that women had to cover their heads in church, it does not mean that Christians have to do likewise for all eternity!

What then makes the message of the Bible universal? How is it that we in twentieth-century North America, or our comrades in post-revolutionary China, can discover in it God's word for our/their condition? For one thing, the Bible is not just a jumble of multi-coloured beads, like marbles in a small boy's pocket. Rather, like a gorgeous necklace, it is connected by a thread which runs through each bead, a thread of over three thousand years of tradition that has been passed on, from generation to generation, in the life of a living community. And that thread is the search for the Promised Land by those whom God has liberated from slavery, a land flowing with milk and honey where all will live with God and the blessings of that life (Revelation 21:1–4); where all will have enough to eat without discrimination between rich and poor (Proverbs 22:2; Isaiah 29:19; Acts 4:34–37; Galatians 3:28); where war, disease, and death have disappeared (Micah 4:3, Revelation 21): in short, the glorious commonwealth of God.

That is the Christian vision of the future, promised by all the Scriptures. Meanwhile, on earth the search continues, manifesting itself in a people who practise justice (Micah 6:8). For to do justly and to love one's neighbour is to know God (Jeremiah

22:15–16; Luke 10:27; James 1:27; 1 John 3:13–18, 4:20). So then, the various strands that make up the Bible are bound together by the life of a historic community, the People of God, who have been liberated by God and called (*ecclesia*, the Greek word for church, means "those who have been liberated and called together") to do God's will. The necklace is bound together, not only as a closed circle, in and with itself, but also as an ongoing revelation, binding us to it through God's continuing call. For us, God's word represents an ever-renewable source of guidance and insight, so we return to it over and over again for help.

But that does not mean that the Bible will grind out ready-made solutions for us without any effort on our part. Quite the reverse. We may read it, or hear it read, and understand nothing (Mark 4:12: cf. Isaiah 42:20). Jesus continually put his hearers on the spot by asking them, "What do *you* think?" (Matthew 15:15; Luke 10:26; and many other places. The whole point of the parables was that they forced people to think for themselves.) In the passage quoted at the head of this essay, Jesus says to his hearers, "Why do you not judge for yourselves what is right?" So ultimately the onus is on us. But not necessarily on us as individuals. It is one of the blessings of belonging to the Christian movement that we have support from our comrades and a tradition from past experience to help us in the search. It may involve struggle. But if our struggle follows the right line—"Seek first God's realm and justice"—then all other matters will fall into place (Matthew 6:33).

For Discussion

1. Can you imagine the background of the three Bible stories quoted in this chapter? (Remember they were written down many years after the incidents recounted in them took place.)

2. Do you think these stories apply to us today?

3. How does our context, here in Canada, help us to understand their meaning for today?

4.   If Jesus identified with weak and marginalized people, how can we follow him?

5.   What do we mean when we call the Bible "the Word of God"?

For Further Reading

Robert McAfee Brown, *Unexpected News: Reading the Bible with Third World Eyes* (Philadelphia, Westminster Press, 1984).

Cho Wha Soon, *Let the Weak Be Strong* (Bloomington, IN: Meyer-Stone Books, 1988).

Raymond Fung, *The Isaiah Vision* (Geneva: WCC Publications,1992).

John Spong, *Rescuing the Bible from Fundamentalism* (New York: Harper-Collins Publishers, 1991).

R. S. Sugirtharajah, ed., *Asian Faces of Jesus* (Maryknoll, NY: Orbis Books, 1993).

Masao Takenaka & Ron O'Grady, *The Bible Through Asian Eyes* (Auckland, NZ: Pace Publishing, 1991). [Asian Christian Art]

4 Where Is God Acting Today? Discerning the Signs

In the Gospels, people were always asking Jesus to show them a sign (i.e., some proof) that he was really engaged in God's mission (Matthew 16:1–4; Mark 8:11–13; Luke 23:8). And Jesus' answer was always the same: "The signs are there. Why don't *you* read them?" In the story that forms the theme of this essay, Jesus used the folk wisdom of his day to show the disciples that they were perfectly capable of interpreting the signs (i.e., of seeing where God was at work) and were "hypocrites" (i.e., fooling themselves; not acting like mature people) if they refused to do so. Let us remind ourselves of this passage:

> Jesus said to the people, "When you see a cloud rising in the west, you immediately say, 'It is going to rain'; and so it happens. And when you see the south wind blowing, you say, 'There will be scorching heat'; and it happens. You hypocrites! You know how to interpret the appearance of earth and sky, but why do you not know how to interpret the present time? And why do you not judge for yourselves what is right?" (*Luke 12:54–57*)

It is interesting to note that the word translated 'interpret' ('discern' in the older versions: the Greek is *dokimazein*) has an "open-ended" sense to it of carrying out a successful experiment. In other words, when we try to understand or interpret the signs of the times, we are not guaranteed success, but that should not deter us from trying. This risk-taking nature of all human action in the world is especially characteristic of Christian activity. To run away from it is to display immaturity ("What hypocrites you are!"), just what Jesus is scolding the disciples for.

The late Professor Caird calls attention to that point in his little Pelican commentary on St. Luke's Gospel. He goes on to explain that Jesus here is urging the disciples to be sensitive to the political atmosphere of Palestine. For Jesus, economic and political factors represented vital elements in the search for God's realm. The coming conflict between the Jewish people and the Roman Empire appeared inevitable (Mark 13:1–8; Matthew 24:1–2; Luke 21:5–11),and Jesus wanted his disciples to think deeply how they would respond. Would they stand firm when figures like Theudas or Judas the Galilean appeared, claiming to be Messiah (Acts 5:36–37; cp. Mark 13:6)?

So those who followed Jesus were to use their God-given common sense to "interpret the present time" in the same way that they were accustomed to foretell the weather. Two thousand years later, we go by the same folk wisdom. But science has now given us much more accurate (though by no means absolute!) tools and techniques for interpreting the weather. And the social sciences, too, can help to analyze what is going on in the world, economically and politically, making it ever more possible for Christians to discover where God is at work. The study of economics and political science and a critical reading of the daily news have, to paraphrase the great German theologian Karl Barth, become a vital part of our daily prayer life. Christians today, if they are to lead a fully rounded spiritual life, cannot afford to do without at least a rudimentary analysis, in terms of their faith, of the social context in which they find themselves.

Some Christians, such as the British historian E. R. Norman, have attacked what they call the intrusion of secular thought into the realm of religion. For them, religion is something spiritual, within us, to do with the individual's personal relation with God. It is something separate from the day-to-day occurrences of life, having to do with the future life in heaven. To confuse the religious and the secular is somehow to sully the purity of our faith.

Such criticisms were answered over fifty years ago by the great archbishop of Canterbury, William Temple. He wrote, in effect, that God is not exclusively, or even primarily, concerned about religion, but about the *whole* of the created order. God feeds the birds of the air and clothes the flowers of the field (Matthew 6:26–30), sending rain on righteous and unrighteous alike (5:45), and knows when even a sparrow falls to the ground (10:29).

How Jesus reflected this holistic concern of the heavenly Creator is revealed in the various temptations that beset him during the time in the wilderness, when he was thinking through the ministry to come (Matthew 4:1–11; Luke 4:1–13). Temptations only have power when they represent real, or important, possibilities. Thus, to demonstrate messiahship by an "economic miracle" (turning stones into bread) which would make it possible to feed starving people would be a real possibility, especially for someone like Jesus who was so concerned about the poor.

That this was an important *element* of messiahship, Jesus demonstrated with the feeding of the five thousand, so important an act that it was one of the few incidents recorded in all four Gospels. But economics, by themselves, can be misused. The ancient Romans understood this when they used "bread and circuses" to distract the common people from their oppression. The over-emphasis on economic determinism in Marxist theory is one factor that has led to the present chaos in Eastern Europe and the uncertain road being trod by China today. So Jesus rejected the exclusive use of economics to bring about the realm of God. But, in doing so, Jesus also pointed to its importance as an element of any just society.

And so with the other temptations, which symbolize the manipulation of political power ("all the kingdoms of the world") or miraculous religion (testing God by going against natural laws like gravity) to achieve messiahship. Politics and religion each represent vital elements in a rounded life. But the exclusive emphasis on one by itself—its use to bribe or seduce people— can lead to a perversion of human life, to fascism or theocratic absolutism. In rejecting such exclusive criteria, Jesus opted for a holistic solution in which each should play its allotted part. And this mission, by its radical character, posed such a threat to the ruling classes of the day that it led to the Cross.

Human beings are often tempted to claim absolute priority for one or another level of life. And in doing so, they reveal their own limitation (the wilful refusal to recognize this limitation we call sin). Our North American society, for instance, emphasizes the laws of the marketplace, and, in so doing, comes close to calling economics absolute (economism). In totalitarian societies, political demands are treated in similar fashion, while in such theocratic societies as Iran or Israel or Burma, religious demands may dominate. In all cases a lopsided and inhuman society results, because God has created all orders to inter-relate. So a world in which this balance exists—the just and holy (holistic) society of God — becomes the aim of all who have inherited the tradition of the Hebrew and Christian Scriptures.

Consequently, when Christians search for God's activity, they may expect to discover it anywhere that a juster and more humane society is emerging. To paraphrase Temple once more, God is interested only incidentally in how fast an institutional church is growing in a given part of the world. To put it another way, for those who believe that God was revealed in the human person of Jesus Christ, the distinction between religious and secular that people such as Norman make does not really exist. God is far more concerned about a world in which people can have fresh drinking water; be liberated from disease, poverty, and war; and live in freedom and creative community to give glory to their Creator. That is what the prophets and Jesus were called to proclaim, and that is the mission that Jesus calls all his followers, from Peter down to each one of us, to carry out (John 20:21).

Today, a whole new emphasis on the economic factors of the marketplace has appeared. Symbolized by the dominance in world affairs of the International Monetary Fund (IMF) and the demand for "structural adjustment" within "developing" economies, it has resulted in a lopsided international situation in which a relative few live in affluence while the majority of the world's population is deprived of basic human needs. And the affluent nations are willing to deploy all their technological might in order to keep the poorer countries in their place. A whole series of armed incidents, from Grenada to the Persian Gulf, manifests this willingness.

Such a New World Order can be described in Christian terms only as sinful. We have usually thought of sin as individual selfishness or disobedience to God's commands. But the world situation today compels us to conclude that this selfishness can result in the formation of entire systems or structures whose nature is to benefit a few at the expense of the many. So sin can be structural as well as personal. This means that the Christian call for repentance and conversion includes the demand to struggle for structural change—for the overthrow of unjust and sinful systems — as well as for deep personal change.

Where, then, does individual conversion fit into this scheme? What about God's care for each one of us and the promise of salvation in Christ Jesus? Are we in danger of stressing the horizontal relations, between person and person, to the neglect of the vertical, between us and God? Where does spirituality come? Surely what we are describing *is* spirituality: the horizontal and the vertical are two parts of one relation. "Love God with all your heart . . . and your neighbour as yourself," says Jesus, and drives this command home by observing that only those who *do* the will of God will be able to say, "Lord, Lord" (Matthew 7:21).

So conversion is an inward turning from self to God. It involves repentance (in Hebrew, the word *to turn* denotes both repentance and conversion) from a life of sin and the beginning of a new life—for the Christian *in Christ*. To put it in different words, Jesus calls each one of us to turn (convert) *from* the self-gratification of consumerism and the idolatry of the market, *to* Christ's way of love for God and solidarity with the poor and disadvantaged (Matthew 5:3–12, 6:19–24). Our eyes that have been blind to injustice and oppression will be opened and the road to eternal life will become clearly seen (Mark 8:23–25). Only then will we be enabled to see where God is at work and how we fit into that plan to change the evil structures that have enslaved humanity (Ephesians 6:12). Only then will we experience the joy and exhilaration of knowing that we follow Christ and do God's will; that we are participants in a mighty movement, in history but over and beyond time and space, of all who work together with the Creator of the universe to establish the realm of heaven. As a distinguished Jesuit, Fr Pedro Arrupe, once said, "What we must reconquer and reform is our entire world. In other words, personal conversion and structural reform cannot be separated."

Wherever God is acting in our world "to dethrone rulers and exalt the poor . . . to satisfy the hungry and send the rich away empty-handed" (Luke 1:52–53), we know that we, by virtue of our baptismal promise to follow Christ, are being called and sent.

Several great movements stand out as contemporary illustrations of God at work in history. Others will become evident as we put these principles into practice. The five listed below are not necessarily in order of importance. All point toward the coming of God's commonwealth here on earth ("your kingdom come, your will be done, on earth as in heaven"); all deserve our participation and support, though we as individuals may have to establish personal priorities.

1.   One is, without doubt, the struggle of the Third World for liberation. Ever since India, led by Mahatma Gandhi, began its epic struggle for independence in 1920, the colonized nations of the world have been striving, in the face of the incredible cruelty and blind power-hunger of the Western colonizers, to free themselves. China's liberation in 1949 under Mao Zedong promised to be an epoch in the quest, though the situation today is marked by ambiguity and uneven progress. Yet the justice of the cause, for instance, of blacks in South Africa, or of peasants and Amerindians in Central and South America cannot be disputed. For Christians in North America or Europe, to acquiesce in any policies of the American, British, or Canadian governments which hinder the activity of these liberation movements means a clear transgression of God's will. We need to maintain an attitude of constant vigilance—to support moves that will help and to oppose those which hinder the cause of liberation. The creation of a juster world, in which the deep gulf between rich and poor nations will be eliminated, represents a top priority for all Christians.

The situation is a complex one. No simple solution has so far appeared to the problem of the way in which North and South have become economically interrelated with one another, perpetuating the inequalities between the two. No better illustration of structural sin in a fallen world exists. Nations like South Korea or Singapore appear to have pulled themselves out of the swamp "by their own bootstraps." Yet in doing so their rulers have opted into the capitalist game, creating new areas of poverty to feed their own affluence. Nonetheless, such countries have shown that it is possible for nations to achieve some measure of self-sufficiency and the question now remains of a juster way that will avoid the poverty and exploitation that have so far characterized the path of development.

2. Related to the liberation movement in the Third World is the struggle for freedom from discrimination on the part of minorities *within* our various societies. Few countries escape such struggles. Mayan Indians in Mexico, Basques in Spain, Tamils in Sri Lanka, or Catholics in Northern Ireland, reveal the explosive potential of these movements. But they do not negate the quieter demands of aborigines in Australia, native people in Canada, or Ainu, Koreans, and *Burakumin* in Japan. Beyond race, the recognition of worth in gay/lesbian relations; or respect for those marked by physical or mental differences; even permission for creative social eccentricity, represent other issues that no mature and democratic society can afford to disregard if it is to be perceived to be obedient to the divine will.

Nor need we be put off by the fact that the leadership of so many liberation movements is not specifically Christian. This development is a good illustration of God's concern for the world, *as a whole*, about which we have been thinking. God is not limited to the Christian church for action in the world: poor God, if that were so! God could choose a great pagan monarch like Cyrus of Persia to liberate the Jews in exile (Isaiah 45:1–6; 2 Chronicles 36:22–23): God can also call Gandhi or Mao or Mandela. They have all done God's will and deserve our praise.

> Thus says Yahweh to the anointed,
>   to Cyrus,
>   whose right hand I have grasped,
> to subdue nations before him
>   and strip kings of their robes
> to open doors before him—
>   and the gates shall not be closed:
> I myself shall go before you
>   and level the swelling hills;
> I will break in pieces the doors
>   of bronze
>   and cut through the bars of iron.

I will give you the treasures of
    darkness
      and riches hidden in secret places,
so that you may know that I am Yahweh,
    the God of Israel, who calls you
      by your name.
(*Isaiah 45:1–3*)

3. The worldwide movement of women for release from their bondage to men, under which they have suffered for millennia, represents a third area of God's activity. Christians have often been accused of providing an ideological justification for patriarchal oppression. The Bible from Genesis on is full of passages (e.g., Genesis 3:16, 1 Corinthians 11:3) which justify the male domination of women, and this bias was further emphasized by the misogyny of the doctors of the church like St. Augustine.

While such a bias reflects Christianity's compromise with the patriarchal nature of Western society it does not explain the almost universal prevalence of patriarchy in other parts of the world. All the great religious and philosophical traditions of the East— Hinduism, Buddhism, Confucianism, Judaism, and Islam—place women on a lower level than men. Yet all, including Christianity, also give lip service to another, more egalitarian, theme. Beginning with the Hebrew Scriptures in Genesis 1:27, and continuing with the Christian in Mark 10:6–9 and Galatians 3:28, there is a recognition in theory of the equality in God's creation of female and male. According to the creation story in Genesis:

God created humankind in God's own image,
in the image of God, God created them;
male and female God created them.
(*Genesis 1:27*)

In Mark's Gospel, Jesus refers back to this old poem, reaffirming it when he says, ''In the beginning, at the creation, God made them male and female.'' And St. Paul further consolidates the tradition when he writes to the Galatians, ''There is no such thing as Jew and Greek, slave and free, male and female; for you are all one person in Christ Jesus'' (Galatians 3:28).

But a sinful society, based on inequality and domination by the strong, has made it difficult until now to match theory with practice. Today, a combination of economic and cultural factors makes it impossible to avoid action in the direction of a new set of social relations. Once more, God calls us to listen to and see what God is doing in society. Once more, the church is being challenged by those outside it to take action.

As with all revolutions, this one will not succeed without much suffering and effort. That so many within contemporary Christianity fail to recognize God's call in this struggle reflects the extent to which the values of a fallen and sinful world have infiltrated God's people (as they have in the church's compromise with economic inequality, racial discrimination, and many other sinful and un-Christian attitudes). Thus God calls those who can hear to a mission on two fronts: to a reform of the church in its patriarchal and hierarchical structures, and to a basic change in the oppressive institutions of society at large.

4.   Fourthly, the peace movement can, without doubt, claim a fundamental place in God's plan for our world. If we are to believe the Sermon on the Mount (Matthew 5, 6, 7), not to mention other sayings such as Matthew 26:52, it would appear that the original movement founded by Jesus was strongly pacifist. And this attitude can still be found as late as the third century, and continues down to the present in the monastic movement, in various pacifist sects, and in the personal stand taken by individual Christians. But as the movement expanded, the church found itself faced with situations that demanded change. We can understand this if we look at the spontaneous and reactive violence that may erupt in the struggle for liberation, particularly in those places where repression by those in power provides a primary structure of violence. Are Christians to stand by and disregard the struggles of comrades who are being massacred by death squads in Central America?

But international war as it has come to be is another question. The calculated planning of mass, even cosmic, destruction, evidenced by Great Power stockpiling of nuclear weapons and the continual threat of their use in such conflicts as the recent one in the Middle East, represents a horrible attempt to play God which no Christian can condone. Can a Christian condone the mass destruction of innocent people so recently carried out in Iraq in the name of a "New World Order"? Events in the Caribbean, in Central America, and in the Persian Gulf have demonstrated that certain elements in the advanced capitalist nations have been prepared to annihilate the world rather than relinquish their hegemony or share with the Third World the affluence they have amassed.

Even for those who accept the Just War argument, such destructive egocentrism cannot be countenanced. So our mission in the near future may well take the form of the kind of civil disobedience practiced in the early church and displayed in modern times by Gandhi, Martin Luther King, or the Berrigan brothers. We may be called to refuse the payment of taxes or to invade factories and military bases where nuclear weapons or other armaments of destruction are stored. Individuals and small groups of Christians are already carrying out such tactics and the movement may spread. Whatever way it may be necessary, we have to make ever more clear the opposition of at least a minority of the North American population to the demonic and irrational plans of its rulers. That such opposition exists and is effective is reflected in recent moves to play down and defuse the threat of nuclear war. But much more needs to be done; for example, in other areas such as "Star Wars" and the international sale of arms. For Canadians, civil disobedience, which appears to break the law, will seem particularly repugnant. But was not Jesus nailed to a cross for breaking the law of the land?

5.   Finally—though by no means completing the list—comes God's call for us to pay attention to what the World Council of Churches calls "The Integrity of Creation." The destruction of our natural environment which has resulted from our inability to understand the implications of a one-sided growth in technology, combined with the irresponsible expansionism of a capitalist economic system, now threatens all life on this planet, not to mention the causing of local conflicts all over the world.

As with the oppression of women, Christianity has been seen

to have justified the unconditional exploitation of nature by human beings. In the sequel to the creation poem in Genesis 1, quoted above, there is a verse which reads,

> God blessed them [the human beings] and said to them, ''Be fruitful and multiply, and fill the earth and *subdue it*; and *have dominion* over the fish of the sea and over the birds of the air and over every living thing that moves on the earth.''
> [Italics mine]
> (*Genesis 1:28*)

The command to subdue the earth and have dominion over all living things has been seen to give us permission to act as if we were completely independent of our natural environment and could exploit it as we wanted. But we can argue that it is the greed of a sinful humanity, not God's command, that drives human beings to exploit creation. The Genesis story may tell us that we humans are the crown of the creative (evolutionary) process. But it also makes clear that we are as much part of creation, and as dependent on the other parts of the natural order, as are the birds and the beasts. To act as if we were autonomous—like God—is sinful (Genesis 2:16–17). Moreover, even those cultures, particularly in East Asia, which see clearly that humans are part of, and dependent on, nature have ravaged their environment badly. The terrible floods that have occurred over the centuries in China are the result of deforestation, while the present plan to dam the Yangtze gorges is causing as much horror among environmentalists as the destruction of the rain forest in the Amazon.

No wonder, then, that Christians have responded to the call of environmentalists in our own country to protect the rain forests of the West Coast. In a part of our land where a huge proportion of the population is dependent on the lumber industry for employment, such action has led to conflict and polarization. It is not yet clear how the problem will be worked out, but the justice of the cause is clear. And this is only one aspect of a situation that includes many other facets—air and water pollution, the ozone layer, etc.,—which are going to demand huge adjustments in the way our present industry and way of living are organized. So we can see that God is here calling us to open our eyes to a part of the mission that we have largely disregarded. Part of the dream of God's new society which appears throughout Scripture, from Isaiah (Isaiah 40, 41) to St. John (Revelation 22:1–5), is the vision of a nature that has been renewed. We are being called to follow that dream.

The call to participate in such movements may seem an odd view of mission to those who have been reared in older and more personal theological positions. Yet, when we contemplate the context in which we live in the light of God's word in the Scriptures, the conclusion is inescapable and has come to be recognized widely within the Christian movement. For instance, a Syrian Christian bishop from South India recently remarked to a North American audience that the apostles did not possess the technological capacity to abolish poverty: we do. Thus the abolition of poverty becomes a moral question for Christians today (i.e., we can do it if we really think it is right. If we do think it is right, but don't do it, we are doing wrong.). Therefore, continued the bishop, it is no longer today a question of evangelizing the unbelievers, but of calling the unjust to repentance.

In the face of such choices, the seemingly overwhelming power of a technological society where control lies in the hands of a few people has driven many Christians to despair. In North America, one dominant trend in religion is toward an authoritarian, otherworldly faith which makes few demands on its followers, except to relinquish their God-given powers of mature personhood. This kind of faith may provide a refuge for the timid and weak of heart. But it has also become the ideological justification for the drive toward a new world order which is so characteristic of the United States today. Its symbols bear little similarity to the gospel of Jesus Christ, resembling rather the story of the scarlet woman in Revelation 17 and 18, with whom the kings and merchants of the earth committed fornication. In that account the writer seems to have been pointing at the wealth and power of Rome, the persecutor of the Christians. But the image for us today can represent any power that has given up the pursuit of justice and human welfare for the acquisition of wealth and power.

Those who have ears to hear the true gospel know that their powerlessness is taken up into God's almightiness. With Mary we rejoice that God has "lifted the humble high." We Christians have been called, as were our first ancestors in the faith, to be a kind of counter-culture; to go out from this world of false values to work out our own vision of what God's commonwealth will be like. As Paul expressed it, we are not to "be conformed to the pattern of this present world," but our minds are to "be remade and our whole nature thus transformed" (Romans 12:2).

Such a conversion to creative non-conformity, involving separation from the world, has nothing to do with the false extricationism of much North American popular religion. It represents, rather, a judgment on the perversion of technology and the economic injustice which characterizes the society in which we live. We pursue a different goal from the children of this world, and we pursue it here and now. We discern God's hand in the liberation of women from subservience to men, or of third-world countries from neo-colonialism. But we cannot remain content with a kind of interior, subjective expression of approval. Our faith demands works.

For Discussion

1. When Jesus asked the disciples, "Why do you not judge for yourselves?" what do you think he expected them to do? What are we, as followers of Jesus, expected to do?

2. How can Christians train themselves, economically and politically, to discern where God is at work in the world?

3. Many people today seem satisfied to live their lives outside the institutional church. Have they ceased to be Christians? Is the church limited to the institution? Can we do without the institution?

4. Can we take part in the eucharist and other religious practices if we are not also engaged in one or another of God's liberating activities?

5. How would you describe sin?

For Further Reading

J. Miguez Bonino, *Room to Be People* (Philadelphia, Fortress Press, 1979).

G. B. Caird, *Saint Luke* (London: Penguin Books, 1963).

Debbie Culbertson, ed., *Freedom from Debt* (Toronto: Ten Days for World Development, 1992).

David G. Hallman, *A Place in Creation: Ecological Visions in Science, Religion, and Economics* (Toronto: United Church Publishing House, 1992).

Elizabeth Moltmann-Wendell, *Liberty, Equality, Sisterhood* (Philadelphia, Fortress Press, 1978).

Project Ploughshares, *The Ploughshares Monitor* (Quarterly bulletin of Project Ploughshares, an ecumenical coalition for disarmament and development) (Waterloo, ON: Conrad Grebel College).

Paul Rogers & Malcolm Dando, *A Violent Peace: Global Security after the Cold War* (London: Brassey's, 1992).

Letty M. Russell, ed., *Feminist Interpretation of the Bible* (Philadelphia: Westminster Press, 1985).

5 Evangelism: What Is the Gospel for Today?

At the risk of oversimplification, let us set up a scheme. If the context in which we live is the age of change, technology (with its blessings and its curses) and revolution, and if our mission is to participate in God's actions in history (whose purpose is to heal the divisions between human beings and Godself), then can we say that evangelism is the proclamation of God's reconciling plan within the context of our age? If that is so, we need to be clear about the exact meaning of our definition of evangelism and especially about two key terms in it.

The first is the word *proclamation*. For most of us evangelism means some form of verbal communication, whether by preaching, or writing, or through the electronic media; something that requires training and skill which only a few of us possess. But that is a rather modern use of the term, coming from its use in an age when printing, radio, and television are so predominant, thus placing undue emphasis on verbal skills. The Greek word *evangelizo*, usually translated as "proclaim the gospel," meant much more than verbal communication. Perhaps a term like "spread the gospel," implying a kind of epidemic action, like spreading a cold, would be more accurate—especially in defining how the gospel spreads most successfully. Wherever Christianity has grown most rapidly—in the church of the first centuries, in Africa or China today—there has been preaching, yes, but most of the work has been done by ordinary, often illiterate folk, whose lives demonstrated Christ's power to change people. We might call it "evangelism by example." As the writer of the Book of Acts has the Risen Christ say, "You will be my witnesses" (Acts 1:8).

The second phrase, *context of our age*, is crucial because it describes the mode of *incarnation* so basic to the gospel, and under which we operate. God's child is born within a certain context of time and place ("under Pontius Pilate" and "under the law"). Jesus lives "as a servant" (the Greek is "as a slave"), the lowest class in society, and is limited by obedience to these historical and cultural conditions. Thus Jesus' proclamation of the gospel represents a response to the expectations of his own people and the traditions which they had inherited.

Consequently, there is a marked difference between the gospel preached by the Palestinian Jesus, and the one proclaimed by the Greek-speaking, Diaspora Jew, Paul, largely because the context differed within which each worked. Let us take a little time to compare the two. First Jesus. Jesus worked within the Hebrew tradition of the prophets and wisdom writings represented by the Baptist, in whose movement he began his ministry. Mark's Gospel records it thus:

> In those days Jesus came from Nazareth of Galilee and was baptized by John in the Jordan. And just as he was coming up out of the water, he saw the heavens torn apart and the Spirit descending like a dove on him. And a voice came from heaven, "You are my Son, the Beloved; with you I am well pleased."
>
> * * *
>
> Now after John was arrested, Jesus came to Galilee, proclaiming the good news of God, and saying, "The time is fulfilled, and the kingdom of God has come near; repent, and believe in the good news."
> (*Mark 1:9–11, 14–15*)

Both John and Jesus were mainly concerned to prepare the people for the coming of God's domain or realm (kingdom) which the Jewish people had been taught to expect since the time of Amos and Isaiah, seven hundred and fifty years before. This was a strongly ethical tradition: that is, it looked forward to a time when God would establish on earth a society where peace, justice, and good relations among people would reign. Luke's account of John's ministry (Luke 3:7–14) reflects the same emphasis on

concrete action that is revealed in Jeremiah, who equated just dealing between king and people with "knowing" (that is, loving
and being loved by) God (Jeremiah 22:15-16). Matthew, Mark,
and Luke all agree that Jesus regarded his ministry as a continuation of this tradition. Luke spells it out, as follows:

> When [Jesus] came to Nazareth, where he had been brought
> up, he went to the synagogue on the sabbath day, as was his
> custom. He stood up to read, and the scroll of the prophet
> Isaiah was given to him. He unrolled the scroll and found the
> place where it was written:
>
>> The Spirit of Yahweh is upon me,
>>   because God has anointed me
>>   to bring good news to the poor.
>> God has sent me to proclaim release
>>   to the captives
>> and recovery of sight to the blind,
>>   to let the oppressed go free,
>> to proclaim the year of the Lord's
>> favour.
>
> [Jesus] rolled up the scroll, gave it back to the attendant, and
> sat down. The eyes of all in the synagogue were fixed on him.
> Then he began to say to them, "Today this scripture has been
> fulfilled in your hearing."
> (*Luke 4:16–21*)

So for Jesus, the gospel was to be proclaimed in terms of the old,
prophetic announcement of the Year of Jubilee which, as we have
seen, was to be a foretaste of the coming kingdom, a time when
all debts were forgiven and inequalities in wealth would be abolished. Accordingly, in his account of the early church in Jerusalem, Luke shows them taking this teaching seriously:

> All who believed were together and had all things in common;
> they would sell their possessions and goods and distribute the
> proceeds to all, as any had need.
> (*Acts 2:44–45*)

and again,

> Now the whole group of those who believed were of one heart
> and soul, and no one claimed private ownership of any pos-
> sessions, but everything they owned was held in common.
> (*Acts 4:32*)

Paul, on the other hand, was called to be an apostle (someone
sent) to non-Jews (Galatians 2:7), whose religious tradition differed
markedly from that of the people of Israel. Salvation for the
intellectuals of the Mediterranean region consisted in the practice of ascetical exercises leading to self-knowledge (*gnosis*). But
this kind of exercise demanded leisure for meditation—and therefore a certain degree of wealth. For the poorer masses there were
numerous popular cults. Although their practices differed in
detail, most involved identification with a dying and rising god
whose gift of new life would release people from their bondage
to evil spirits and to the fate in which they were entangled. Jesus'
death and resurrection fitted rather well into this pattern, so well
that Paul was able to proclaim, as he did in such great works as
his letter to the church in Rome, that we could be saved by faith
in Christ Jesus:

> Now the words, "it was reckoned to him," were meant to apply
> not only to Abraham but to us. It will be reckoned to us who
> believe in the God who raised Jesus our Lord from the dead,
> who was handed over to death for our misdeeds, and raised
> to life for our justification. Therefore, since we are justified by
> faith, we have peace with God through our Lord Jesus Christ.
> (*Romans 4:23–5:1*)

In the First Letter to the Corinthians (1:22–24), he puts it a
little differently:

> Jews demand signs and Greeks desire wisdom, but we proclaim
> Christ crucified, a stumbling block to Jews and foolishness to
> Gentiles, but to those who are the called, both Jews and Greeks,
> Christ the power of God and the wisdom of God.

And finally, in 2 Corinthians 5:18–19, we are given a further summation:

> All this is from God, who reconciled us to Godself through Christ, and has given us the ministry of reconciliation; that is, in Christ God was reconciling the world to Godself, not counting their trespasses against them, and entrusting the message of reconciliation to us.

Of course, all this doesn't mean that Paul lost sight of the ethical emphasis. His concern for economic equity between Greek-speaking and Palestinian Christians (2 Corinthians 8 & 9) demonstrates this fact. Above all, in his great passages on life "in Christ" (Romans 12, Colossians 2:6–17 and dozens of other passages in which he expounds the nature of Christ's social body, the church) he points up the change in behaviour that becoming a Christian (living "by the Spirit") brings about in a convert's life. But the way he begins his message differs from Jesus' strong proclamation of repentance and the kingdom. As Luke pictures him preaching to the Athenians (Acts 17:16–34), Paul begins, not with the coming of God's realm, but with "Jesus and the Resurrection."

So, each time Christians faced a new culture they tried to shape the proclamation of the gospel so that it could be heard as good news to those people. When missionaries went from the Mediterranean world to northern Europe the same change took place. There Christ was proclaimed as a dying hero, something the warlike Teutonic tribesmen could understand. When Pope Gregory the Great sent Augustine to England, he urged him to respect any indigenous religious practices and places of worship, just as long as they did not contradict the spirit of the gospel. That is why we find so many of the great churches of Europe (e.g., York Minster) located on the site of ancient pagan sanctuaries.

Today, Minjung theology in Korea is shaped in terms of the old stories of the common people's longing for justice and freedom from oppression. And liberation theology in Latin America reflects the same process of adjustment. The missionary listens for the way in which the people express their hopes and fears. In the response Jesus is always the centre, but *how* the good news of Jesus is presented varies according to the questions the particular culture has raised concerning life, death, injustice, and other fundamental problems of life.

There have been certain instances when Christianity did not respond to the "cry of the people" in a certain culture; when the gospel came as something so exotic that it appeared incapable of being understood. In such cases the Christian community has tended to die out, or else to remain a little enclave of devotees to a foreign cult. This was the case with the Nestorian Christianity which entered China with the silk trade over thirteen hundred years ago. It flourished for several centuries, as long as contact with its western source was maintained. But it never succeeded in jumping over the barrier of Chinese culture and was swallowed up by Buddhism, an equally foreign import but one which seemed to have been able to respond better. In our own day this has also been the case with Japan where Christianity, after over 400 years, has remained locked within a middle-class, intellectual shell, never able to attract more than one per cent of the total population.

Because so many missionaries in modern times proclaimed the gospel without first submitting themselves to the questions raised by the culture in which they worked, without listening to the "cry of the people," the gospel has often gone unheard and the seed fallen on barren ground (Mark 4:3–9).

So evangelism will not be a simple task. For both Jesus and Paul, as for the prophets before them, the gospel came as judgment before it came as good news: there was nothing cheap about it. The kingdom is like a pearl of great price for which we must be willing to give up, if necessary, everything that we have (Matthew 13:45). "Is not the day of the Lord darkness and not light?" thunders Amos to the rich people of Israel. "Repent!" says Jesus, "the Kingdom of God is upon you." For unless we repent—that is, change our ways—we will not be able to receive the gospel.

This coupling of repentance with gospel represents an important truth for those of us who live in North America, most of whom have to minister in a context of middle-class affluence. The good news can come to us only after we have altered the middle-class lifestyle we live as North Americans, a lifestyle that has resulted from our pillage (or at least the pillage by our forebears) of the Third World and of the native people and poor of our own land. The gospel promises us freedom from the alienation and sense of powerlessness from which most of us suffer, but only after we have come to understand the sinful and illusory nature of the idolatrous worship of technology and conspicuous consumption which we in Canada take for granted.

What then will be the gospel which we will proclaim in response to the fears and expectations of our age and culture? Here we have to pause and think. If the old Christian missionaries can be accused of not listening to the "cry of the people" in the cultures to which they were sent, it is equally possible to say that we in Canada are not very sure what it is our people are looking for. In the eighteenth century, when most people were emerging from feudalism, with its strong corporate emphasis, they were seeking a sense of each one's individual worth. So when John Wesley and the other evangelicals and pietists preached the love and redeeming power of Jesus Christ for each individual, thousands flocked to hear that good news.

Today, Billy Graham and the Lambeth bishops continue to reiterate the same gospel. In places like Africa, where people are emerging from tribalism, the message has power. But in North America, individualism has run its course and each one of us feels alienated from our neighbour. Dr. Graham has been rejected by the majority of his own denomination who now believe that he is flirting with liberalism. Only those who stand politically and theologically to the right of him continue to enjoy success. So, in spite of the Decade of Evangelism, Anglicans in the West, most of whom do not accept fundamentalism, continue to decline in numbers.

So how are we going to frame the gospel of the love of God in Jesus Christ in a way that will be heard as good news by North Americans? We shall have to do a lot of listening before we can give solid answers. And we also have to remember that every proclamation of the gospel has to be phrased in a way that people will be able to grasp. In past ages certain slogan-like "catch phrases" have emerged which people remembered and carried with them. For the time of Jesus it was "The kingdom of God is near"; for our forebears, "Jesus is Lord," "Jesus loves you," "Accept Him as your personal saviour," and so on. These are all expressions people heard and treasured as descriptions of a much greater complex of faith. Perhaps it is still too early for us to coin our own expressions. They have to develop out of our practice and preaching to be truly successful. So what follows will be only a few hunches, to be tested for acceptance or rejection.

1. *A Gospel for the Affluent.* To follow Jesus means a life in which we shall work for freedom from violence (nuclear war, wife- and child-battering, rape and mugging in the streets, family instability); freedom from economic instability (unemployment, inflation, high rents and real-estate prices, uncontrollable economic cycles); above all, release from the sense of alienation and powerlessness. So we need to proclaim a new society where each can participate in the political process and in basic economic decisions which affect our lives. This is the true worship of God.

Does this gospel sound too materialistic? Quite the opposite. If we follow the analysis that has preceded these pages, we shall realize that all the woes we have listed here (and with which we are so familiar) are the results of a world where people have turned away from God to trust in economic and technological processes and the consequence is the enslavement of human beings. Only when we realize that we have been enmeshed in that demonic system of power can we seek God's grace to escape from it. No multiplication of expensive and simplistic, televised, evangelistic programs will help us do anything but turn away from the responsibility God is laying on us. Only action to change this society into one that is in greater accordance with God's will can bring us the hoped-for liberation.

2. *Poverty in the Midst of Plenty.* A million and a half people go without work in this country, laid off in the name of restructuring, while those at the top continue to enjoy high salaries. Over two million live below the poverty line, with thousands homeless in our cities, while another four million are considered functionally illiterate. Because of the spread of automation in office and factory, there seems little hope that unemployment (which has increased every decade since the end of World War II) will disappear. That is the dark side of our affluent society, where the gap between those who have enough and those who live in poverty widens yearly. Is this God's will?

Moreover, inequality in Canada represents just one section of a worldwide pattern. Our country occupies part of that twenty per cent of the world which monopolizes eighty per cent of the world's resources. The eighty per cent of the world's people must make do with twenty per cent of the energy, food, and other materials available for use. Because of this imbalance, at least five million will die of starvation this year in north-central Africa alone, in a world where science and technology have made it possible for all to have enough.

Christian missionaries have been warning for over half a century that relief alone, without long-term structural change and the alteration of unjust trade patterns, would not improve the lot of the poor, but only increase their dependence. It is these poor and starving whom Jesus said would inherit the kingdom of Heaven. What is the gospel we proclaim to them today? "Go in peace, God loves you," we say (James 2:15–16), but do little to feed or clothe them. The leaders of Cuba, Nicaragua, China, and Zimbabwe held out for their people a vision of a new society where, as the psalmist sang, "there will be abundance of corn in the land." That their success in material terms has been minimal can be explained in part by their lack of experience in democratic practices and the underdeveloped nature of their economies. But deliberate sabotaging of their efforts by such policies as the United States blockade of Cuba or the support of Contra forces in Nicaragua has done much to ensure failure. In Africa, the system of trade laid down by the GATT agreements in 1993 will continue to make any economic growth in the lands south of the Sahara difficult. Where exactly do we stand on these questions? What is God's will for us in this situation?

As we have seen, the maintenance of a pattern of economic injustice in the world is one of the aspects of a sinful and fallen world. Accordingly, preaching repentance and conversion will include, for North Americans, a willingness to change such structures, even though that may be to our short-term disadvantage. Such willingness will include our assent to movements for auton-

omy and economic self-sufficiency in third-world countries, movements which might result in a lowering of our own standard of
living. Western reaction to recent events in the Middle East and
Somalia show that our part of the world is far from willing to
assent to such change.

3.   *Racism, Classism, and Sexism.* Do we think that we worship
God in a land where our native people go poor and landless, and
immigrants are discriminated against (Matthew 5:23–24)? Can
we say that we love God when women feel the oppression of a
society dominated by men; when males even monopolize God
by making "him" male, in their own image? Do we really believe
that in Christ there is neither Jew nor Greek, slave nor free, male
nor female? How well do our churches mirror that vision of the
new heaven and new earth, in canon law, in ordination, or even
in the make-up of our congregations? The gospel for today must
include the promise of healing for these sores on our social body,
not only in some future life, but also here and now. Note well
that Paul uses the present indicative—"there is"—, not some future
tense—"we hope there may be"—, in his words to the Galatians
quoted above (Galatians 3:28).

4.   *A Life on Two Levels.* Finally, the gospel which we preach
will promise a life to be lived on two levels, but the two will inter-
mingle and interact so thoroughly that it may be difficult to distinguish between them. The first level is faith in a future promise
of life "in Christ": the vision of a Promised Land where we shall
be released from the bondage of those structures and values which
govern this world (2 Corinthians 4:18). In following this vision
we leave "the pattern of this present world," as Abraham left
Haran, without any surety that the future will be as we hope
(Hebrews 11). This is the necessary level of spirituality: of prayer
and meditation and worship. Without it, a Christian cannot live.

This spirituality is lived out on a second level, in the constant
struggle to bring this world and its structures into line with God's
will for God's commonwealth of justice, freedom, and peace. Each
change in society which results in greater reconciliation between
races, truer equality between sexes, or less inequity of possessions,
is a change that accords with God's will, whether it has been

↳ Still must discern this will

accomplished by Christians or not. Every attempt to obstruct such change, even if it takes place in Christ's name (as our leaders in church and state often attempt to do), is against the will of God. That is our gospel.

How then do we proclaim this gospel? Here we return to what was said about proclamation at the beginning of this chapter. The English missionary-theologian Roland Allen wrote a book years ago entitled *The Spontaneous Expansion of the Church*. In it he pointed out that Christianity spread most rapidly in the early centuries of its history, when expansion was spontaneous; that is, when it was carried out by hundreds of nameless Christians, each relating to her or his neighbour, rather than in the consciously organized way that has been characteristic of the modern missionary movement.

Tertullian, a Christian scholar of the second and early third centuries, had a saying, ''We are not much good at talking, but we live!'' In other words, the most effective evangelism consists, not in sermons, radio, or television shows; that is, in talking or preaching, but in the kind of lives that ordinary Christians live; in a lifestyle that reflects real freedom, integrity, and joy in a world where dishonesty, fear, insecurity, and tension are the rule. Lives that have been ''renewed and transformed'' form a counter-culture of non-conformity which points to a new way for those who are oppressed by the old. One ancient Christian writer after another has backed up Tertullian's testimony, telling how they were converted by the integrity and sense of true community exhibited by the church in their time.

Let us end with a few concrete illustrations of what a Christian counter-culture might be like.

1. *A Spirituality of Nonconformity.* The old spirituality which we inherited from the Christianity of medieval Europe, which was based on monastic life, stressed personal self-cultivation which looked toward final salvation in a future heaven. This ''privatized'' faith conformed very well to both the individualism and the compartmentalization of life in a modern industrial society, where faith (considered as something personal) must not be allowed to interfere with business (considered as a public duty).

The "old" spirituality emphasized the otherworldly nature of our calling. The world in which we live is a world of sorrow and sin. But we could look forward, through the merits of Christ's death, to joy in heaven. In Sunday school I was taught that texts such as, "My kingdom is not of this world" (John 18:36) meant that God's kingdom was something that we would experience only after death, in heaven. All we could do was dream, as it were, about the joys we would experience there. As we contemplated in our worship the mystery of the Altar, we might be given some glimpse of that glory. As Bernard of Cluny wrote in his famous hymn, "Jerusalem the golden,"

> I know not, O I know not
> what joys await us there,
> what radiancy of glory,
> what bliss beyond compare.

This "old" spirituality, though still offering much to its practitioners, is rapidly expanding in two directions. It has become more this-worldly in its commitment "to take up our cross (that is, to become an opponent to the *status quo*) and follow Christ," here and now. In other words, it has become a spirituality of creative nonconformity.

The new spirituality sees the break between Christ's kingdom and the kingdom of this world to exist, not primarily between this life and the next, but here and now, in a difference in goals. If this world sees the attainment of power and wealth—being CEO of General Motors, a house in Oakville or Westmount—as a worthy goal, the Christian sees identification with the poor and marginalized as the height of what it means to be spiritual (to be "blessed" Matthew 5:3). This identification often brings Christians into conflict with their society. This is the case of the bishop of San Cristobal de Las Casas in Mexico, who chose to support the Mayan revolt in Chiapas against an oppressive society in January 1994. He made clear that he did not agree with the violence of the rebellion, but agreed even less with the unjust laws that were driving his people off their ancestral land.

Needless to say, Christian opposition to the status quo means something much deeper than simple opposition to present government and economic structures, though it will often include that. Jesus was executed by the Roman power as a revolutionary ("King of the Jews"). But there is nothing in the Gospels to indicate that he ever planned an armed rebellion. The threat he posed to the leaders of his day, both in church and state, consisted in his steady refusal to accept their standards of authority (tradition, hierarchy, patriarchal power). The common people heard him gladly (Mark 12:37) because he taught with a different kind of authority from that of their scribes (Matthew 7:29). "Call no one father," he said (Matthew 23:9,11), "The greatest among you will be your servant." Under a God who is love, leadership consists in serving that God and the neighbour made in God's image. So the cross we are to take up represents the criticism—even ostracism, in extreme cases even martyrdom—we are to be prepared to receive if we follow in that Way.

Secondly, the new spirituality stresses a more corpoate, shared—and also ecumenical—nature, focussed on the celebration of the eucharist and Bible study together, within the context of the struggle.

For Christians the eucharist is an act of worship and an acting out of what it means to live in God's commonwealth of freedom and justice. It is the heart that keeps alive and growing the community of Christ's Body. In this liturgy people who have been carrying on their own respective work in the outside world, bring that work to be offered at God's table under the form of bread and wine. But both their work and what is offered are made imperfect, both by individual shortcoming and by the sinful structures of the world in which they have been carried out. Only by being taken into the perfect self-offering of Jesus Christ on the cross can they be cleansed and offered to God. In communion we receive back the bread and wine, now Christ's Body and Blood. There we become "one body as we partake of the one bread." And we are sent out into the world once more to carry on Christ's mission within our daily tasks.

This kind of spirituality has already begun to appear in the house churches of China, in the Minjung theology of South Korea, and in the Basic Christian Communities of Latin America and the Philippines, or in movements like the Sojourners in the United States. It is being worked at by members of the Christian coalitions (not to mention countless other, more informal, small groups) here in Canada, who have designated its conscious formulation as a top priority.

Each one of us needs to work at some form of it for ourselves and our particular community, in terms of our own particular social context. We are nonconformists because our long-term goals differ from those of the world around us. But we also need to be creative because the social situation in which each one of us exists is different. What are the needs of those around us who are suffering or disadvantaged? Just where can we carry out our mission "to bring good news . . . and to proclaim release"? A spirituality of creative nonconformity represents a most basic element in our evangelism today.

2.   *Consumer Resistance.* One form that this creativity might take is consumer resistance. In his work, *The Apostolic Tradition*, the third-century Roman theologian, Hippolytus, lists a number of ways that those preparing for baptism—and of course, all Christians—were to demonstrate that they were following the New Life. Refusal to attend the gladiatorial games, or to offer incense to Caesar (an act of pagan worship), rejection of military service and other state-related forms of employment: a whole catalogue of prohibited practices has been drawn together. On a more positive note, these novices were to be willing to be marked out by the police when they visited Christian comrades in prison or took food and clothing to widows and poor people. All these were ways that followers of the Way became known (i.e., proclaimed the gospel) to those around them. Other contemporary writers affirm that witness, often linking such practices with their own conversion. By showing that they were not afraid to act differently from the accepted ways of pagan society, Christians made their faith known.

A few centuries later, when Christianity was accepted and the church grew rich and powerful, many committed Christians left the cities for the desert, where they practised a life of asceticism and poverty. As time passed this movement coalesced into what we know today as the Monastic Movement. But not all of its members became monks. Many of the great leaders of the day—St. Athanasius, St. Basil, St. Jerome, and St. Augustine, to name only a few—joined this movement and brought its values back into public life.

Consumer resistance can be an important way in which we today demonstrate our adherence to a new set of values based on the gospel. "Life is more than food, the body more than clothes," taught Jesus (Matthew 6:25). Good food and nice clothes are part of gracious human living, but their use has been perverted in our society by turning them into ends (i.e., goals for the whole of life) rather than means (i.e., things which we can use) for a fuller life. So Christians can practise owning fewer goods; avoid "impulse buying," and emphasize quality of life over unlimited acquisitions. Two reasons for adopting this practice are: 1. consumerism is a basic principle on which the society we oppose functions, and 2. that society is now beginning to crumble. Like those who joined the monastic movement during the declining days of the Roman Empire, we will be able to provide an alternative model for living in a world of declining employment and overall standard of living.

Of course, we need to draw a distinction between such resistance and blind (superstitious) hostility toward *all* science and technology and its products, such as has characterized some counter-cultural movements in recent times. We oppose the *perversion* of science and technology, most of all the way it has chopped up truth and set group against group. But we also recognize God's hand (the blessings) in the discoveries themselves. And we would like to integrate them into a more holistic (holy, divine) world view. So just how we are to act out our resistance and nonconformity in concrete terms is still far from clear. That is why we need to be creative in thinking our programs through, each according to the context in which we find ourselves.

3. *Elimination of Sexism and Paternalism.* St. Paul wrote (and believed) that "in Christ we are all one person: there is no such thing as Jew and Greek, slave and free, male and female" (Galatians 3:28). He worked hard to abolish the distinction between Jew and Gentile (racism) in the Christian movement, but we still have difficulty with racial discrimination. It took another eighteen hundred years before slavery could be abolished, and we still find class distinctions hard to deal with. Now at last we are coming to realize that female has been subordinated to male, just as slaves were formerly owned by free people. This subordination has probably existed from the beginning of written history, though there are hints that more equal societies were to be found in prehistoric times.

Certainly Christians believe that both male and female were created in the image of God, and modern New Testament scholars like Elizabeth Schussler Fiorenza and Leonard Swidler argue that Jesus treated women on the same level as men, restoring God's purpose to our human existence. Woman's subordination within the church developed as the Christian movement made compromises with contemporary society, just as it allowed economic inequalities to creep in.

In our day, God is calling us to abolish this distinction that a sinful humanity has introduced. Although Christianity in the Third World has pioneered in establishing women's rights, in our own society the church often finds itself behind the community at large. Worse still, it invokes the Christian tradition to justify this oppression. Christ had some hard words for people who obstinately twist and pervert God's commands: "Whoever slanders the Holy Spirit can never be forgiven; they are guilty of an eternal sin," he said (Mark 3:29). And in another place (Matthew 21:31) Jesus warns that people on the fringe of society, like tax collectors (racketeers?) and prostitutes, would go into the kingdom of Heaven ahead of church people who only pretended to do the will of God.

In this connection one wonders what Jesus would have said about our contemporary heterosexist marginalization of gays and lesbians, both in and out of the church? Matthew's Gospel (19:12) records an obscure but tantalizing little saying which runs something like this:

For while some are incapable of marriage because they were born so, or some were made so by men, there are others who have renounced marriage for the sake of the kingdom of Heaven. Let those accept it who can.

Jesus' main point here concerns those like himself (and later, St. Paul and many others) who chose a celibate life for the sake of their mission. But in the course of doing so he refers to other forms of celibacy. The one "made by men" clearly refers to the barbaric practice in the ancient world of creating eunuchs by castration to oversee women in their quarters (the harem), and so forth. But what the first reference means is far from obvious. Scholars show by the way they have translated the passage—some literally, some figuratively—that they had difficulty in making up their minds. But one thing is clear: there is not the shade of a hint of judgement against those who were "born eunuchs" (i.e., for whom a heterosexual relationship has no meaning). Indeed they are spoken of in the same sentence with those who have "renounced marriage for the sake of the kingdom of Heaven," a status that has always been held among Christians in the highest honour. That such a judgement would be hard to accept is clear from the concluding statement, "Let those accept it who can."

To return to our main point, the submission of women is without doubt an intrusion into the Christian movement from a fallen, secular society which stresses patriarchy. We of the creative counterculture need continually to be aware lest our own standards become conformed to the pattern of this age. Only by continual struggle (men listening to women, both sexes to gays and lesbians, etc.) can we preserve our honesty. Our proclamation of the gospel must be unequivocal to be heard.

4. *Human Worth.* As we have seen, technological society tends to subordinate human beings to machines, while capitalist society places balances in account books ahead of people. For the Christian, however, human beings have been made in God's image, only one step removed from Godself (Psalm 8:5). To subordinate them to any system is equivalent to blasphemy. Yet instances of discrimination and subordination abound in all of our societies and are used to the advantage of those in power. War and genocide, as with Western support of right-wing murder squads in Latin America and the Philippines, treat people as pawns of giant corporate interests, without worth in comparison to the vested interests of states and multinational corporations.

In contrast, the Christian counter-culture, with its nonconformist spirituality and holistic world view, will practise unlimited reverence for human worth. Yet a continual struggle takes place between the two sets of values. Even for the converted, basic attitudes have been formed in a tightly organized society based on hierarchy, patriarchy, discrimination, and subordination, whether of women, native people, foreigners, the poor, the elderly, mentally and physically handicapped people, gays and lesbians, and so on. Thus, unconscious attitudes of discrimination or superiority will persist with relentless tenacity. That is why we have to die continually to that old nature and be raised with Christ to a new humanity. In other words, we have to be helped, through association with those who are discriminated against, to discover and root out those unconscious attitudes in ourselves.

5.   *Pacifism and Civil Disobedience?* As Western society feels an increased threat from the Third World, the danger of local wars escalating into major conflicts will become greater. Christians need to consider a more overt opposition to the gigantic arms stockpiling being practised by the major powers. Even with the end of the Cold War and various tentative deals to disarm nuclear weapons, the armaments industry continues to receive a disproportionate segment of our national budgets. Arms sales to other countries bring in huge profits and contribute to the continuation of local wars in places like Somalia or the Balkan states. As church coalitions like Project Ploughshares remind us, the need for vigilance about peace is still vital.

Some Christian counter-cultural groups are practising civil disobedience in the form of withholding taxes and other strategies. Philip Berrigan, a seventy-year-old Roman Catholic, was recently arrested for leading a party of four into a U.S. air force base to pour blood on an F–15E bomber (one of the type used in the bombing of Iraq). Such actions will inevitably bring counter-cultural Christians into conflict with others, even within the church itself, who appeal to a kind of perverted faith in order to support the policies of the state. So, as it was in Nazi Germany, Christians may find themselves opposing Christians. As Jesus observed, we find our enemies under our own roof (Matthew 10:36).

In such a situation, counter-cultural Christians will have to take care not to yield to the temptation of becoming an inturned, self-justifying sect, distinct and cut off from the community within which it resides. Historically, the church has always resisted such tendencies. It has chosen rather to function as a leaven, that is, as a movement *within* society. Jesus' original description of Christians as salt, or yeast, implies that the movement, by its very nature, will be able to influence society as a whole. Thus it is natural that they should be involved today with non-Christians in so-called secular movements like the peace movement, movements for native rights, and the women's movement, all of which struggle for the achievement of human worth. That is the way we can proclaim the gospel most effectively.

Christians who have experienced the joy of living in a free and equal counter-cultural community will naturally want to see similar values established in society at large. Our knowledge of God and obedience to Jesus Christ demand it. In a world where God offers vast blessings for all humanity; where science and technology make it possible for us to make those blessings real, but in a world where that same science and technology pose a threat to the very survival of the human race, God calls the church to bear witness to the reconciling love revealed in Christ Jesus. Whichever path we choose, the blessing or the curse (Deuteronomy 30:19), will determine the truth of the gospel we proclaim.

For Discussion

1. Have you heard the "cry of the people" in Canada? What are they saying?

2a. Are there unemployed people in your parish?
  b. What can we do about homeless people? About poverty in general?

   c. How many immigrants do you think Canada can admit each year?

3. Should the right to self-government for native people be written into the Constitution?

4. What do we mean, in concrete terms, by "creative counter-culture"?

5. When a division arises over the question of evangelism within our congregation (or the church at large), how will we work that out?

6. Is civil disobedience an option for Canadian Christians?

7. When people look for spirituality today (as they do), what are they seeking? Is this something that Christians can respond to?

8. What are the unique features of a Christian spirituality?

For Further Reading

Rafael Avila, *Worship and Politics* (Maryknoll, NY: Orbis Books, 1981).

Anthony Bellagamba, *Mission & Ministry in the Global Church* (Maryknoll, NY: Orbis Books, 1992).

Robert McAfee Brown, *Spirituality and Liberation* (Philadelphia: Westminster Press, 1988).

R. McAfee Brown, ed., *KAIROS: Three Prophetic Challenges to the Church* (Grand Rapids, Michigan: Eerdmans, 1990).

Tom Harpur, *Communicating the Good News Today* (Hantsport, NS: Lancelot Press, 1987).

John F. Kavanaugh, *Following Christ in a Consumer Society: The Spirituality of Cultural Resistance* (Maryknoll, NY: Orbis, 1981).

Kenneth Leech, *The Eye of the Storm: Living Spiritually in the Real World* (New York: HarperCollins, 1992).

Douglas Macdonald, *The Politics of Pollution* (Toronto: McClelland & Stewart, 1992).

James O'Halloran, *Signs of Hope: Developing Small Christian Communities* (Maryknoll, NY: Orbis Books, 1991).

Working Group on Gays and Lesbians and the Church, Anglican Church of Canada, *Our Stories/Your Story* (Toronto: Anglican Church of Canada, 1990).

Other Books on Anglicanism
from the Anglican Book Centre

Anglican Essentials
Reclaiming Faith in the Anglican Church of Canada
George Egerton, editor
1-55126-095-6

Anglicanism and
the Universal Church
Highways and Hedges 1958-1984
John Howe
with an overview 1984-1990 by Colin Craston
0-921846-30-4 paper 324 pages

Aspects of Constitutional History
The General Synod of the Anglican Church of Canada
H R S Ryan
1-55126-037-9 paper 148 pages

Authority in the Anglican Communion
Essays Presented to Bishop John Howe
Stephen W. Sykes, editor
0-919891-61-6 paper 286 pages

Resolutions of the twelve Lambeth Conferences 1867-1988
with an Introduction by Owen Chadwick
Roger Coleman, editor
0-921846-44-4 paper 320 pages

The Eames Commission: The Official Reports
The Archbishop of Canterbury's Commission on
Communion and Women in the Episcopate
Robert Eames, chairman
1-55126-101-4